FROM PROMISES TO PROGRESS:

A leadership guide to help organizations bring their racial equity aspirations to life

Andrew Beamon

Preface

The day I walked across the stage for my high school graduation was the moment I decided I wanted to go to college. I know, it was a pretty last-minute decision. My father had been trying to talk me into going for some time, but I did not believe I was college material. The majority of Black students from my high school were not going off to college after graduation, while the majority of white students were. I thought he was crazy to gamble his money on what I thought was a bad bet because I honestly hadn't shown any academic interest or achievement since the 7th grade. The day after my high school graduation, we drove up to Eastern Connecticut State University (ECSU) and met with the President and Vice President of the university. My uncle was friends with both of them, and to my surprise, they were both Black men. Meeting both these men, who were leading this university, challenged my thinking on what "college material" looked like.

A few days later, I moved into the dorm at ECSU to attend their 6-week STEP CAP program. This program was for students with poor grades or low SAT scores. If you passed this 6-week boot camp, you were automatically admitted. There were about 25 other students, and most were Black too. Here I met some of the most brilliant students that only needed to learn the right study skills and have a safe learning environment. I attended ECSU for only one full year before transferring to and graduating from North Carolina Central

Preface

University (a Historically Black College & University in Durham, North Carolina) in 2002. That summer boot camp program at ECSU and attending NCCU were pivotal to my personal growth and love of learning.

I share this story as an example of how powerful seeing Black representation and being exposed to Black excellence is in young people's lives. Seeing a few Black people from my community go to college gave me some confidence that I could do it. But seeing two Black men, Dr. David Carter and Dr. Stanley Battle, lead a state university, and then going to North Carolina Central University, where almost every member of the staff, professors, leadership, and students were Black, was transformational. It was meaningful and inspiring. I gained more confidence in my academic ability than I could ever have imagined. I was freed from what Ibram X Kendi, author of "How to be an Anti-Racist," called biological racism: The act of expressing the idea that races are meaningfully different in their biology, and that these differences create a hierarchy of value. I was freed from the thought of one group being more "book smart" than the other. It changed my perspective of myself, my definition of Blackness, and the trajectory of my life.

I was undergoing my own personal transformation in college, but afterward I still had to enter back into the cold reality of society. At a Historically Black University, Black youth are fairly safe from racial abuse and discrimination, but not when they leave the community. After college, I thought I was mentally prepared to deal with racial discrimination, but I honestly didn't have the experience to address it well in the workplace. My experiences dealing with racism in the workplace started immediately with my first job at 16 years old, which isn't much different from what other Black people in America experience. Managing overt and covert anti-Black racism is a part of the job and is the Black workplace experience. Getting prepared for racism in corporate America is similar to when my cousin got me mentally prepared for riding a motorcycle. He said it is not about if you will fall off the bike, and it's a matter of when you will fall. All bike riders fall. It's a part of the expected experience. You will be hard-pressed to find anyone that rode motorcycles not sharing stories about the time or times when they fell on their bikes. They will show each other their scars, and talk about the moments of danger. I always listened closely because I wanted to find a way to avoid a terrible bike accident. I have a cousin who seriously injured his knee, and I also have a cousin who lost his life in a bike accident. On the road you have to watch out for the drivers that don't see you and others that don't have your well-being in mind. As an early biker, it was a stressful experience knowing that one bad mistake by myself or someone else could result in my body hitting the pavement. The danger was real, but through experience I began to relax and reduce the fear. And yes, I fell a few times, but my scars healed, and I could walk away from the accidents.

This expected experience is the same in the Black community when experiencing racism. This danger is also real. Many Black professionals share these stories of confronting racism in the workplace. It's never an "if" you will experience anti-Black racism; it's

Preface

"when". I always wanted to find the best ways to reduce these opportunities for racial acts against my colleagues and me at work. In my case, over time, the attempts to avoid acts of racism in the workplace resulted in social isolation. The thought process was the less I interacted with co-workers, the safer it would be.

In 2009, I traveled to Nebraska for the first time for my new job's onboarding program. My classmates in the onboarding cohort were getting ready to go out to the bar to hang out after training. One of my classmates knocked on my door and asked if I was going with the group. I told her I wasn't going because I wanted to read and prepare for tomorrow's class. She continued to extend the invitation. No matter what excuse I gave not to go, she had a solution for it. Finally, I felt I had to be open and honest with her. I told her I had just started with the company, and I wanted to make sure I didn't get into any trouble. She was confused and said, "What trouble?" I explained it was my first time in Omaha, Nebraska, and I don't know how the race relations were in the bars or clubs here. I didn't think it was worth the risk of running into the wrong crowd, having a confrontation, and losing my job. She replied, "Wow, I never would have thought of that." We agreed that she would feel the place and the other classmates out, and the next month I would go out with them when we returned for part two of the training. I'm happy to say, I went out the next month and I had a safe time and didn't run into any trouble.

We both learned from this experience. My colleague had only been in America for less than two years, was of Indian descent, and wasn't truly aware of the anti-Black racism that still existed in 2009. Whether she thought I was irrational or not, I appreciate that she acknowledged and respected my concerns. Unfortunately for her, a few years later after joining a new company, she told me she was witnessing the sad reality of overt racism against Black people at her new workplace.

I learned from her that isolation is not the answer, and there was no way I could continue like this in corporate America. What was I avoiding by not going out to the bar or socializing with my co-workers? Was my fear of having a negative experience with a classmate or a random person at the bar irrational? Was I overreacting by thinking I would be fired if I was attacked and defended myself?

Based on my personal experiences encountering racism, maybe it wasn't an irrational fear. I experienced aggressions from a co-worker that would refuse to shake my hand, a customer calling me racial slurs, a senior leader referring to me as Toby from Roots. My stories are not unique. Like the experiences of Driving While Black and Shopping While Black, Black people are also aware of the stress of Working While Black.

Through a lot of practice, I got much better at navigating and managing racism in the workplace. However there still is a mental, emotional, and political dance or chess match being played. But the question is, why should I have to learn how to exist in a toxic environment? Why did I have to be coached by my parents, uncles, cousins, and colleagues on how to best address anti-Black racism? I would prefer an environment where that's not the norm.

Opportunity: To better Equip leaders driving Racial Equity

I want to think beyond teaching techniques and designing survival kits for Black people to manage racism at work. Why can't we put some of that energy into eradicating systemic racism from the workplace, and be change agents? We shouldn't just accept this as an unchangeable circumstance. Let's work on building a new reality.

Often, when people talk about racial inequities, it is usually explained away by detractors as if racism is not the primary reason or barrier. People point to other causes like education, poverty, or family structure.[1]

After the murder of George Floyd, detractors had a hard time explaining things away as not race related. The demonstrations in the streets gave companies a call to action to combat anti-Black racism. There was nowhere for corporate America to hide. Large companies scrambled to develop a strategy to better support their employees, customers, and society as a whole. Companies began taking a stance against racism and making promises to do better within their organization. Regardless of motive, whether it was the brand's reputation, pressure from stakeholders, or a genuine concern to

---

[1] Badger, Emily et al., "Extensive Data Shows Punishing Reach of Racism for Black Boys." The New York Times, March 27, 2018.
https://www.nytimes.com/interactive/2018/03/19/upshot/race-class-white-and-black-men.html?mtrref=search.yahoo.com.

correct mistakes, companies began looking for diversity, equity & inclusion strategies and executives in droves.

Diversity, Equity & Inclusion, Social Impact, Environment Social Governance (ESG), and Corporate Citizenship are all fairly young and growing fields where there aren't many people with the executive experience companies are searching for. At the start of 2019, only 47% of S&P 500 index companies had a Chief Diversity Officer (CDO) or equivalent, and just two-thirds of those were hired or promoted into those roles in the past three years.[2] According to Tina Shan Paikeday, leader of D&I Advisory Practice at Russell Reynolds Associates, 63% of diversity chiefs in the S&P had been appointed or promoted to their roles within the past three years [3]

With the demand being so high, if companies cannot pull a senior DE&I executive from another organization, they will most likely end up with someone new to this role. Large organizations like Apple, Netflix, Microsoft, Zoom, and Facebook will not have a hard time winning the war of DE&I and Social Impact talent, but what about everyone else? This leaves most organizations with one option. They have to train new leaders quickly on bringing racial equity to life.

"Diversity Management" is covered pretty well in hundreds or maybe thousands of books today, but there is a lack educational

---

[2] McGirt, Ellen. "Chief Diversity Officers Are Set Up To Fail." Fortune, December 19, 2019. https://fortune.com/2019/03/04/chief-diversity-officers-are-set-up-to-fail/.
[3] Cutter, Chip, and Lauren Weber. "Demand for Chief Diversity Officers Is High. So Is Turnover." WSJ, July 13, 2020. https://www.wsj.com/articles/demand-for-chief-diversity-officers-is-high-so-is-turnover-11594638000.

material focused specifically on implementing racial equity in the workplace. **This book aims to dispel the myths and provide practical solutions to help executives design a more effective playbook and avoid severe missteps while building an anti-racist, purpose-driven, culture.**

This is for the employees who have suffered from racial discrimination and inequity, and all other forms of oppression inside and outside the workplace. Those that wake up every day trying to bring their best selves to work while encountering overt and covert racism, microaggressions, unconscious bias, disrespect, and policies and procedures that negatively impact them and their family.

It is also for DE&I practitioners that have the overwhelming task of balancing the needs of the organization and employees, managing all aspects of diversity, and are tired of seeing the unique experience of Black colleagues be ignored. This is also for the executive trying to implement anti-racist policies and programs within their organizations and community.

Questions for Reflection

1. When did you first experience racism in the workplace?
2. Why do you believe racial equity is necessary in the workplace?
3. What are the biggest needs and challenges of addressing anti-Black racism?
4. What experiences, courses, or books prepared you most for racial equity work?
5. How would you rank your readiness to drive racial equity on a scale from 0-10?

Contents

Preface iii

Chapter 1: Is This Still America? 1

Chapter 2: Diversity, Equity & Inclusion Training and Development 14

Chapter 3: Black Representation...30

    Part 1: Power and Cultural Change 30

    Part 2: The Talent Pipeline Myth 48

Chapter 4: Talking About Race at Work 64

Chapter 5: Cultural Heritage Month Events & Celebrations 79

Chapter 6: Black Community Engagement - History and Current State 87

Chapter 7: Shaping the World for the Better 101

    Part 1 - Institutional and Economic Power..........................101

    Part 2 - Political Power 112

Chapter 8: Repurposing Successful Models and Frameworks to Address Anti-Black Racism 121

Chapter 9: Putting It into Action 136

Appendix: 2020-2021 List of Corporate Racial Equity Actions 145

Acknowledgements 152

About the Author 152

Chapter 1

Is This Still America?

"This is America"

— **Childish Gambino**

In 2020 when George Floyd was murdered in broad daylight on camera, the public couldn't believe their eyes and became outraged. In 1992, when the Rodney King beating was caught on tape, America was shocked that cops would viciously beat an unarmed Black man in the middle of the street. When Martin Luther King was assassinated, we also thought this racist violence could not still be happening in 1968. Over the past 50 years, we have continued to wonder how this can still be happening and whether there will ever be progress.

My uncle, Samuel Beamon, who served as a Marine for 19 months in Vietnam as a Helicopter Crew Chief, also asked, "Is this still America?" when he returned from his tour of duty. In the spring of 1969, he attended his Marine buddy's wedding in New York and was met with the realities of racism:

Excerpt from Samuel Beamon's book, Flying Death:

Everything was fine, until we reached the front door of the clubhouse, where the reception was being held. I was stopped at the door and was told that I could not go in. I reached for and took out my invitation to show it to them. I was then told that I did not understand. Blacks were not allowed in the club. I was in a state of shock and dumbfounded. I felt like I had been stabbed in the back. Was this really America, the same country that I fought for? This is the same country that my friends had died serving. Needless to say, I was the only Black person invited to the wedding and reception. After the Civil Rights Movement, Civil Rights Act and countless demonstrations things were still the same...

I was mad and hurt all at the same time by the attitude of these people, but they would never know it. I was standing near the door, trying to think about how I was going to get into the reception. Several marines came outside to see why I didn't come inside and what the problem was. I told the marines what was said and they were not very happy... After several minutes, one of the marines looked out of the front door. He waved to me to come on in. There were some disapproving stares at me by the managers and staff, as I entered the building and walked into the ballroom. Nothing was said directly to me... After the weekend was over, I learned that the marines had told the management they were going to tear the Country Club apart, if they didn't let me in there. My fellow Marines, My Brothers, had stood up for me. I was proud of them for taking this stand for me. Then again, why should they have to take a stand for me – I was an American, just like they were – or was I? The Constitution of the United States says that all men are created equal, but it does not say that all men are to be treated as equals. This was just another part of the learning process – being a Black man in America – The Double Standard of living in this country.

His story and those of many others are a reflection of the real America. Black people have made positive contributions to this country, even with all of the barriers put in their way at all levels – system level, group level, and individual level – and still face unequal treatment. Despite this, the allies like Sam's marine buddies that acted when they saw injustice, gives people hope for progress and reconciliation.

The Power of Allyship

When Sam's marine brothers saw systemic anti-Black racism, they didn't ask to be better educated on why it was happening. They didn't spend their time sympathizing with Sam or even scheduling a meeting with the country club's board of directors. They acted to disrupt the system.

Fifty-one years later, in 2020, we witnessed acts of disruption by the sports world in the U.S. and worldwide. Starting with the Milwaukee Bucks refusing to play an NBA playoff game in protest against the shooting of Jacob Blake. Followed by the WNBA, MLB, and other major sports leagues around the world. The two-time major tennis champion, Naomi Osaka, announced she would not play in protest, which caused the entire Western & Southern Open to pause.[4]

We also witnessed the power of allyship in small, predominately white communities in the U.S. White people, young and old, marched down their streets to protest in support of justice for Black lives. Small towns like Old Saybrook, Connecticut, stopped business in their town to protest. Author and journalist, Ta-Nehisi Coates, shared a conversation he had with his father during the 2020 protest in a Vox.com article, "I asked him if he could compare what he saw in 1968 to what he was seeing now. And what he said to me was there was no comparison… The idea that Black folks in their struggle against the way the law is enforced in their neighborhoods would resonate with white folks in Des Moines, Iowa, in Salt Lake City, in Berlin, in London – that was unfathomable to him in '68, when it was mostly Black folks in their own communities registering their great anger and great pain. I don't want to overstate this, but there are significant swaths of people and communities that are not Black, that to some extent have some perception of what that pain and that suffering is. I think that's different."[5]

---

[4] Maine, D'Arcy. "Naomi Osaka Won't Play in W&S Semi in Protest of Jacob Blake Shooting; Tourney Pauses Play." ESPN.com, August 27, 2020.
https://www.espn.com/tennis/story/_/id/29749495/naomi-osaka-play-ws-semi-protest-jacob-blake-shooting-tourney-pauses-play.

[5] Klein, Ezra. "Ta-Nehisi Coates on George Floyd, Police Protests, and Hope." Vox, June 5, 2020. https://www.vox.com/2020/6/5/21279530/ta-nehisi-coates-ezra-klein-show-george-floyd-police-brutality-trump-biden.

When we want change, actions matter. The question is, how much are we willing to sacrifice for change? It is always a risk when you act against social injustice. The marine buddies, sports stars, and even people in the small suburban communities stepped up and used their power and influence to help drive change. Who would've thought the act of sports stars not playing and white people from the suburbs protesting would strike that same amount of fear in the U.S. government and corporations as the 15 young marine Vietnam veterans did to the country club manager and staff? Yes, this is still America. Racism still exists, and people are stepping up and making sacrifices to combat it. The death of George Floyd created a great awakening in America and throughout the world that hasn't been seen in 50 years.

Before this, the closest moment of hope for progress around race relations in my lifetime was when Barack Obama was elected president. I didn't know anyone in the Black community that believed a Black person would ever be elected president of the United States in their lifetime. It was just unimaginable that the majority of voters in America would ever vote for a Black president. That election confirmed for me, at the time, that America was making progress. No way would this have happened in 1968. However, we didn't anticipate the unintended consequences of Barack Obama's presidential election – the myth of the Post Racial Society Movement.

Looking in the Mirror #1: The Myth of America's Post Racial Society

Despite the overwhelming statistics on the difficult experiences of Black America, which include health disparities, mass incarceration, lack of economic mobility, and much more, many Americans believed we eradicated racism in 2008, and that we needed to move on to solving other diversity issues. As a result, many Diversity & Inclusion leaders became silent about the Black experience within organizations.

But why did so many people think that America had eradicated racism and that Black people had an even playing field when it comes to employment, justice, healthcare, education, and all other aspects of being an American citizen?

When President Obama was elected, we continued to hear this new narrative of "entering a post-racial America". Many people saw a Black Family in the White House and some Black billionaires – Robert Smith, Oprah, Dr. Dre, and Michael Jordan - and saw this as proof that racism was eradicated. They thought that if they were Black and found success, all Black people could do the same. President Obama addressed this post-racial society myth in his farewell speech, stating, "There's a second threat to our democracy – one as old as our nation itself. After my election, there was talk of a post-racial

America. Such a vision, however well-intended, was never realistic. For race remains a potent and often divisive force in our society." [6]

The second reason people began believing in this post-racism society is the growth in acceptance of inter-racial marriage. According to the Gallup World Poll, Americans have drastically shifted their opinion regarding white and black marriage. In 1968, when asked, "Do you approve or disapprove of white and black marriage?", only 17% of white people approved, and only 56% of Black people approved. The last time this question was asked, in 2013, white approval had increased to 84%, and black approval had increased to 96%. [7] The assumption is that this metric would be a leading indicator of America entering a post-racial society. It seems to make logical sense. If the majority of the country would approve of something as intimate and personal as marriage across races, of course it could equate to people being more willing to recruit, hire or promote Black people in the workplace, which is a much less intimate relationship. Unfortunately, it did not. Approving, or being tolerant, of the behavior and choices of others doesn't always mean a change in your own behavior. Just because a person is okay with Black and white people living in the same neighborhood doesn't necessarily mean they are willing to do it too. Nor does it mean that they will be okay with

---

[6] Business Insider Nederland. "Kijk hoe Obama uitlegt dat een 'post-racial' Amerika onrealistisch was," January 11, 2017. https://www.businessinsider.nl/barack-obama-race-relations-united-states-2017-1?international=true&r=US.

[7] Gallup, Inc. "Race Relations | Gallup Historical Trends." Gallup.com, July 1, 2022. https://news.gallup.com/poll/1687/race-relations.aspx.

renting their home to a Black person or doing business with someone of another race.

Looking in the Mirror #2: Racism is the Primary Cause of Economic Disparities

Progress has been made, but we still have a lot of work to do here in America and across the globe. Yes, some Black people won Emmys, became fortune 500 CEOs, astronauts, and even lived in the White House, however, the African-American community is still dealing with many of the same issues in the workplace and society that they dealt with in 1968. According to the Pew Research Center Survey, I'm not the only person who believes we have a long way to go to improve race relations. In 2019, 58% of respondents said race relations in the U.S. are generally bad, and many see racial discrimination and less access to good schools or jobs as a major reason Blacks may have a harder time getting ahead.[8] And it's not only seen in public opinion polls; racial discrimination has also been shown repeatedly in behavior.

The New York Times article, "Extensive Data Shows Punishing Reach of Racism for Black Boys", shared a study, led by researchers at Stanford, Harvard, and the Census Bureau, that followed the lives of 10,000 Black and white boys who were born between 1978 and 1983 and grew up in rich families and grew up in poor families. For those growing up in rich families, most of the white boys raised in

---

[8] Horowitz, Juliana Menasce, Anna Brown, and Kiana Cox. "Race in America 2019." Pew Research Center's Social & Demographic Trends Project, September 22, 2021. https://www.pewresearch.org/social-trends/2019/04/09/race-in-america-2019/.

wealthy families remained rich or upper-middle-class as adults, but Black boys raised in similarly rich households did not. For poor children, the pattern switched. Most poor Black boys will remain poor as adults. White boys raised in poor families fare far better.

As the New York Times points out, the study debunks several widely held hypotheses on the cause of racial disparities. Gaps persisted even when Black and white boys grew up in families with the same income, similar family structures, similar education levels, and even similar levels of accumulated wealth. The study even eliminates cognitive ability as a possible cause. The article goes on to say, "if this inequality can't be explained by individual or household traits, much of what matters probably lies outside of the home - in surrounding neighborhoods, in the economy and in society that views Black boys differently from white boys, and even from Black girls."[9] If this study debunks myths about the causes people used to explain away the economic disparities between Black and white boys, then what is the primary reason Black males face more significant barriers to economic mobility than white males? The article does point to the specific ways black boys experience racism and discrimination as a possibility. For example, they referred to Black boys being more likely to be disciplined in school and pulled over, detained and searched by the police.

---

[9] Badger, Emily, Claire Cain Miller, Adam Pearce, and Kevin Quealy. "Extensive Data Shows Punishing Reach of Racism for Black Boys." The New York Times, March 27, 2018. https://www.nytimes.com/interactive/2018/03/19/upshot/race-class-white-and-black-men.html.

This study does highlight what many Black people already know and have experienced. There are many contributing factors to the disparities in America, but racism (individual and structural) is the primary driver of inequality. To reduce the disparities in America, our community, and the workplace, we must clearly identify the problem. We have to agree on what we are fighting against. In the workplace, we are still explaining away the racial disparities of the recruiting pipeline by saying it is due to lack of education, years of experience, or leadership development. Why is there racial inequity in your organization's recruitment, onboarding, performance evaluations, promotions, retention, and employee experience surveys? What does it take to stand up for every human being and provide a fair place to work and live?

Hope for Change: Society Has Pushed Corporate America to Respond... Again

Most of the time, organizations have made excuses around why they are not willing or able to help eradicate racism and fix the damage done from racist practices and policies. The reasons usually revolve around their lack of awareness that racism is still a significant factor, not having the funds or resources to address it, or saying the problem is too complex for their organization to solve. However, the external pressure from society put all of the excuses to rest. In 2020 it was clear if an organization wants to do something, they will find a way. When COVID-19 hit the U.S. hard in March 2020, businesses pivoted programs and transformed processes at rapid pace. In less than a month, companies figured out how to work remotely with workforces they previously thought could never work remotely because it was too complicated to manage. Corporate response to the COVID-19 crisis showed us that even complex problem can be solved when they make it a priority.

Yes, Racial Inequity in America Is Real

The artist Donald Glover, also known by his rap name, Childish Gambino, released the music video "This Is America" on YouTube on May 6, 2018, and it had over 12 million views on the first day. This music video won in the Best Music Video category at the 61st Grammy Awards and three years later had over 750 million YouTube views. The video artistically displayed the struggles of so many people in America and around the globe. It unpacked issues of racism in America and instantly broke viewing records, because it resonated with the public.[10] A vivid reminder that despite the progress made, racism in America is still alive and well, and the post-racial society was just a myth.

The myth of the post-racial society also applies to the workplace. According to the Society of Human Resource Management study from the 2008 Global Diversity and Inclusion: Perceptions, Practices, and Attitudes, "some H.R. professionals were already acknowledging the existence of discrimination based on race in the workplace, and many knew barriers were blocking Black employees from opportunities. 21% of H.R. professionals felt that discrimination based on race or ethnicity exists in their workplace.

---

[10] ChildishGambinoVEVO. "Childish Gambino - This Is America (Official Video)." YouTube, May 6, 2018. https://www.youtube.com/watch?v=VYOjWnS4cMY.

41% of Black HR professionals and 13% of White HR professionals agreed. In the same study, 41% of all H.R. professionals said their organization is not doing enough to provide opportunities for Black employees. 68% of Black HR professionals agree, 35% of white H.R. professionals agree".[11]

Many H.R. professionals were already aware of the corporate workplace's role in discrimination and systemic racism against Black Americans and their lack of interest in changing. But unfortunately, the majority wasn't onboard. It wasn't until the summer of 2020, where it felt as though the majority of H.R. professionals and other corporate executives were acknowledging the existence of systemic racism in corporate America. However, merely recognizing there is racial inequity in America, and adding a task to the checklist isn't enough.

Misguided and misinformed efforts will only lead to more stagnation and regression. At this point, we should all be tired of companies doubling down on the same tired and failed diversity strategies. Let's explore the common mistakes and look for better methods to improve the Black corporate experience.

---

[11] SHRM: Global Diversity and Inclusion: Perceptions, Practices, and Attitudes (Alexandria, VA 2009).17

Questions for Reflection

1. What are some of the societal barriers in the way? And how does it impact your workplace?

2. Why are you optimistic that racial equity can improve? Do you have any examples of allyship?

3. What are some examples of demonstrations or real actions you participated in to stop racial inequity or disrupt anti-Black racism?

Chapter 2

Diversity, Equity & Inclusion Training and Development

"If the only tool you have is a hammer, everything looks like a nail"

— **many philosophers**

On April 12, 2018, two Black men were arrested at a Starbucks in Philadelphia while waiting for an associate. The Starbucks manager wanted them to buy something right away, but they decided to wait for everyone to arrive. As a Starbucks customer, I know the manager's request was odd because I've never seen anyone be bothered to buy anything while sitting for a meeting or working from their laptops. This manager, Holly Hylton, called the police on them for trespassing within 2 minutes after the men arrived. This horrible act of racial discrimination was caught on camera and went viral instantly, with over 9 million views in only four days. In the video, you could hear the other customers asking the police why they were arresting the two Black men and defending the gentlemen by stating they weren't doing anything to be arrested for. Protests and calls for a boycott of Starbucks multiplied quickly. In response to this incident, Starbucks not only issued a weak apology defending the store manager, but also pointed to better training as the solution when they stated, "... Our store manager never intended for these men to be arrested and this should never have escalated as it did. We also will further train our partners to better know when police assistance is warranted."[12]

This response did not satisfy Philadelphia protesters or the broader community. After five days of protest and social media posts demanding for the store manager to be fired, Starbucks said it was a mutual decision for her to leave Starbucks, and that they would do more training. Afterward, Holly's history of calling the police on customers was uncovered. When she became the manager, there was a considerable increase in calls to the police. Holly's excessive calls to the police on customers was not a one-off issue. This was a systemic issue that Philly police and the Starbucks district manager allowed to happen at the store. Racial discrimination was business as usual at this location.

The manager's behavior was wrong, but more importantly, the system allowed it to happen. Nobody checked her behavior, so of course, she was going to think her response was acceptable. At Starbucks and other retail or food service companies, someone should be tracking and investigating these types of incidences. For the safety and well-being of your customers and employees, if the number of calls to police doubles at one of the store locations, this

---

[12] 6abc Philadelphia. "Starbucks Apologizes after Video of Arrest in Philly Store Goes Viral," April 16, 2018. https://6abc.com/starbucks-arrest-philadelphia-viral/3342007/

should be a red flag. It's either that the location suddenly became very dangerous, or your team is misusing the police. Either way, there should be a system in place to address it and someone holding the manager accountable.

Starbucks hesitated to do the very thing people were asking for to remedy the problem - fire Holly. Instead of investigating the broken system and the lack of accountability, they decided to implement, the headline-grabbing, company-wide Diversity & Inclusion training initiative. On April 17, 2018, they announced their plan to close their 8000 locations to provide racial bias training on preventing discrimination in stores on May 29 for all of their employees.[13] I don't know what their curriculum consisted of but I certainly hope they learned when police assistance is actually warranted, and I hope their training was followed up with the adoption of a system to monitor police calls and racial discrimination at stores.

I've also experienced getting kicked out places by people like Holly Hylton. I recall an incident at a lounge in Washington DC, where an event manager tried to get security to throw me out. The event was coming to an end, and they closed the back bar where I had a tab for the one drink I had. The security guy told me the back bar section was closed, and I had to wait until the place cleared out. I

---

[13] Starbucks Corporation. "Starbucks Convenes 2,000 Retail Leaders from Across U.S. and Canada to Enable Leadership Excellence as Company Reinvents for the Future." Starbucks Stories, January 20, 2019.
https://stories.starbucks.com/press/2018/starbucks-to-close-stores-nationwide-for-racial-bias-education-may-29/.

patiently waited as everyone left the event and asked the event manager if she could get my credit card from the back bar. After I asked twice, before I knew it, two security guys began dragging me out of the establishment. As I was being pulled out, I said, "really, you're throwing me out for asking for my credit card back." The security guys stopped. Both were Black men. They replied, "you're waiting for your credit card?" with a confused look. I explained the situation to them. They brought me back to the event manager, and I received my credit card after about five more minutes of arguing with her and another employee. They accused me of everything in the book other than actually having a credit card left at the bar. This event manager did not want to take the time to go to the back to get my credit card for me and instead decided it would be much easier to lie about me and tell the security to kick me out. If the security guys had not taken the time to listen to me, the incident would have gone a lot differently. Unlike those Starbucks police officers, those two guys listened to my side of the story. Unfortunately, these incidences are way too common. I admire the two Black gentlemen arrested at the Starbucks, Rashon Nelson and Donte Robinson, for keeping their composure throughout the entire situation. That's not as easy as they made it look. Salute to these Kings.

This Starbucks incident of anti-Black racism sparked a conversation, and I hope other company leaders were listening closely. If you have 8000 stores across America, what do you think are the chances an incident like this occurring at one of your stores? What would have been your response and solution to address the problem? While many items could be discussed around this incident, I would like to examine training for this chapter. Training seems to be the go-to whenever an issue arises, from police shootings of unarmed Black men to discrimination in corporate America against employees and customers. Does racial bias training, like the Starbucks day of training, have a significant impact on preventing acts of racism against Black people? Do these off-the-shelf corporate diversity training, unconscious bias training, racial bias training address systemic racism? These are the billion-dollar questions.

Is Training an Overused Solution to Address Acts of Racism?

According to the Harvard Business Review article, "Why diversity programs fail," billions of dollars have been spent trying to improve diversity representation at organizations, but they have seen minimal results. The article points to mandatory diversity training as one of the leading causes of ineffective programs. It argues that today's training emphasizes the legal case, singles out certain groups to fix, feels remedial, feels like a punishment, and triggers anger and resistance. Some leaders have begun using this article to completely support their plan to stop investing in diversity training programs altogether.[14]

Although I disagree with stopping diversity training as a whole, it has become apparent that organizations are overusing training as their solution to address diversity or systemic racism. And it also

---

[14] Harvard Business Review. "Why Diversity Programs Fail," December 13, 2022. https://hbr.org/2016/07/why-diversity-programs-fail.

appears that decades of diversity, equity, and inclusion (DEI) trainings haven't gotten the positive results we hoped.

The issue is that training is the most readily available tool for leaders, especially DEI leaders, and it is often their only tool. When your only tool is a hammer, everything looks like a nail. Some leaders don't have the power to change the system, but they have control of training and development. As a result, they run to "training" as the solution for every diversity issue that occurs. Training is overused because it is readily available at most organizations, has high visibility, helps protect companies from future legal actions, and could shift the blame from the system to the individual act of an employee.

Company-wide training studies say it could be argued that employees know more about racial bias after the training and that there are sometimes positive effects to employee behavior, but they only last a few days. And this is about it for evidence of a positive effect on organizations. Despite the limited evidence of training having a meaningful impact, U.S. companies keep spending billions of dollars while the status quo remains.

The counterargument is that all types of workplace leadership trainings struggle to produce meaningful change, not just diversity training. The reason for the poor results is explained well in the Fishtank Metaphor. The Institute of Systemic leadership explains, "Wise owners do not blame the fish for their poor appearance or performance. They do not take the fish out from time to time to give them a spot of training, tell them to smarten up and look more lively, and then plop them back in the same dirty water. Instead, they clean the tank."[15]

The dirty fish tank metaphor is the act of taking a fish out of a dirty tank, cleaning it up, and then returning it to the dirty fish tank. This is essentially what most workplace trainings are doing. They are removing employees from a toxic work environment for a day or two, providing them with some new skills and knowledge, then returning them right back to the same work environment and wondering why nothing has changed. Cleaning the "fish tank," aka the "organization's system," is the actual work. Training alone without systemic change has led to minimal positive impact at best, which is wasting billions of dollars in the DEI industry and harming its credibility as a practice.

Let's rethink using training as the solution because, honestly, even some of the most recognized DEI firms have poor training. I recall having a major, well-respected DEI consulting firm provide training for an organization I previously worked for. We had all of our leaders go through mandatory unconscious bias training. This training was very vague, remedial, and the presenter lacked the necessary skills. I recall the presenter telling a story of when he had a moment of unconscious bias that made me cringe. The presenter, a white man, said that he met another white man that had his head shaved bald, and that he immediately got scared because he thought the guy was a member of a skinhead white supremacist group. I asked

---

[15] Rowland, Edward. "Cleaning the Fishtank: A Systemic Lens on Purpose-Led Leadership and Organisations." The Whole Partnership, February 24, 2020. https://www.wholepartnership.com/cleaning-the-fishtank-a-systemic-lens-on-purpose-led-leadership-and-organisations/.

the presenter, "What else happened that made you assume this?" to allow him to elaborate, but he stuck to his story and said, "it was only the bald head." I looked around the classroom, and there were multiple senior white men with bald heads. His odd story continued with him and the bald man having a conversation and realizing that he was a lovely guy and wasn't a white supremacist. That was the opening of this half-day training, and it didn't get much better.

Pamela Newkirk's phenomenal book, *Diversity Inc.* sheds light on the failed promise of the diversity industry and training. Newkirk brilliantly examines the research done on diversity training.

She found that the workload and demand for diversity training may be high, but the practice is plagued with many problems—starting with the quality of training. Newkirk also shared an example from a Chief Diversity Officer, who recalled a poor mandatory training that began with the presenter stating, "In the jungle, there are elephants and giraffes. They are very different but they must get along."

The second issue is the limited evidence of success. Newkirk also shared that a study of 800 intervention workshops to reduce bias couldn't find any empirical data to support that the workshops successfully broke down stereotypes and encouraged empathy.

Lastly, most diversity trainings aren't even trying to address anti-Black racism. Today trainings have a "Diversity for All" approach instead of a social justice approach. Newkirk explains further, "Today's respect for difference of all kinds has overshadowed race and has helped maintain the systemic underrepresentation of people of color who in addition face discrimination due to their gender, LGBTQ identity, physical and mental incapacity, and class."[16]

These studies highlighted by Newkirk begs the question, are executives aware of this failure and ready to change? According to SHRM's June 2020 survey:

- 52% of organizations are adding (or plan to add) new diversity training
- 49% are adding (or plan to add) additional training
- Only 25% plan to add new policies
- 30% plan to adjust existing policies to reduce systemic and structural bias.

Half seem to be doubling down on training. Instead of trying a new tool, they are just buying a bigger hammer. After close to four decades of DEI training, most corporate diversity training as we know it has been a waste of time and money. 25-30% of the organizations acknowledge that you can't just train racism away and realize that addressing the organization's policies and systems is the most effective path to meaningful change.[17]

---

[16] Newkirk, Pamela, Diversity Inc.: The Failed Promise of a Billion-Dollar Business. (2019)

[17] Society of Human Resource Management: Together Forward @Work, "The Journey to Equity and Inclusion". https://togetherforwardatwork.shrm.org/wp-content/uploads/2020/08/20-1412_TFAW_Report_RND7_Pages.pdf

Shifting from the Current One-off Diversity Training to Leadership and Personal & Professional Development

In 2018, I went through a 6-month Strategic Diversity & Inclusion Management Certification at Georgetown University. I saw this life-changing program make a difference in my work and my classmates. Why can't this be replicated in the workplace? One of my conversations while writing this book was with Sukari Pinnock, the founder and director of Georgetown's Strategic Diversity & Inclusion Certification Program and a DEI Training Consultant. When I asked Sukari about her recent experience as a Diversity Equity & Inclusion consultant, she told me:

> *As I've been working with organizations that have contacted me with the intention of doing something around DEI, what I think they really should stop doing is holding the belief that there is a turn-key way in which to get this work done. That there is a series of training that people could go through, books they could read, or other mediums they could consult that would suddenly mean the organization as a whole has done it, and has arrived. Reinventing yourself is going to take time. It is a journey. The work would be changing and ongoing. It's not something where we come in and do 6-8 hours of work together and suddenly the organization will be reinvented in terms of the way it operates around issues of Diversity, Equity and Inclusion…Organizations try to quickly move right into some type of action, and when they do, 80% of them have to go back and they'll have to do something else because the action they took didn't actually get them where they wanted to be. So often times they miss*

making contact because the action they took was not responsive to the need in the moment.

I believe, and my colleagues that practice DEI believe, that the work we are about is really developing adults. Developing individuals so that they could start to understand, what are my values and world views. A lot of times you'll talk to people and you ask them, what are their values and world views, and they just haven't given much thought to it. And most organizations really can't even tell you what their values are......We don't call it training, we shifted our mindset away from that notion. We're not trying to train people to sit, like training animals, we are trying to develop human beings so that they are able to make contact with other human beings understanding that the goal is not necessarily to be in agreement but to be able to hear what the other person is saying, understand that perspective, and at least to be committed.

If there is a shift, I would suggest that we stop thinking about this work as being training, and more as being developmental, personal development, professional development work. In order to start seeing any kind of shift we have to devote a minimum 50 hours of this development work. So when I see videos of people that say we have done 8 hours of bias training and it didn't work, well because 8 hours is not going to shift somebody who has a lifetime of a belief system that they are working with.

Sukari and other great DEI practitioners know that 8 hours isn't enough to make a significant change in an individual, and certainly not an entire cultural change in an organization. We saw a meaningful change in our work after completing our executive certification at

Georgetown University because it was over 120 hours of development (not training), during those 6 months.

Solutions to Make Diversity, Equity, and Inclusion Development Programs More Effective

Even though diversity training has its flaws and is misused by companies very often, I am absolutely not advocating for the banning of DEI development. Instead, I aim to reimagine what training & development to address anti-Black racism, and systemic racism, could look like. The list below are steps you could take to improve your impact.

1. <u>Only use mandatory training if it is tied to a large company-wide system change</u>. Training could be an excellent way to spread awareness and education to prepare employees for a new system change that addresses the diversity issue you aim to solve. I recall introducing a new process to a nonprofit organization where we added new diversity metrics to the chapters' rating system. It didn't go over well with the chapters because they never had any meaningful conversations about the need to increase the racial or gender diversity before this day. Educating people on why diversity matters to your organization before introducing a significant DEI-related process change is a good practice. Understanding drives integration and inclusion.

2. <u>Consider bringing in university faculty</u>. DEI training is not the type of training just any corporate learning & development instructor could teach. The current training

dances around the issues of racism, and social justice, and feels remedial because many of the corporate instructors don't have a deep understanding of the history of racism in America.

3 <u>Invest in your executives and DEI leaders</u>. In order to be prepared to do this emotionally draining work of combating anti-Black Racism and changing the system, your leaders need more than a one or two-day course. Leaders need high-quality education because they will be responsible for identifying gaps and required changes. There are high-quality, 6-month, Strategic D&I Executive Certification programs held by Georgetown University and Cornell University. Invest in all your leaders (not just diversity leaders) with internal and external development opportunities.

4 <u>Implement ongoing external training seminars and conferences for employees</u>: It's a large workload and burden to solve the race and diversity problems in the workplace, and it can't be done by the DEI practitioner alone. Your company should encourage all employees to add DEI to their list of professional development conferences. This work gets lonely, and peer networking could mean a world of difference.

5 <u>Promote experiential learning through community volunteerism</u>: Studies show 70% of your knowledge is from your experience, 20% is from developmental relationships, and only 10% of education comes from classroom training. The Center for Creative Leadership article on the 70-20-10

rule of leadership development states, "(It is) a research-based, time-tested, classic guideline for developing managers, the 70-20-10 rule emerged from over 30 years of our Lessons of Experience research, which explores how executives learn, grow, and change over the course of their careers."[18] For your DEI initiatives, you should partner with your Philanthropic and Volunteerism department and leverage the opportunities to create a meaningful community volunteering learning experience for your employees. This community impact experience could consist of hands-on volunteerism, pro bono volunteerism, helping senior leaders get placed on nonprofit boards, or reviewing grant applications. As you strive to create an anti-racist workplace culture, providing opportunities for your employees to interact with community members from different backgrounds could be a transformative experience for your team.

6. <u>Promote experiential learning by serving on a diversity taskforce:</u> Pamela Newkirk highlighted Coca-Cola's work in creating a diversity task force to monitor progress and hold the company accountable. In the book *Diversity Inc*[19], she relates the findings of researchers Dobbin and Klalev: "Task forces are the trifecta of diversity programs. In addition to

---

[18] Staff, Leading Effectively. "The 70-20-10 Rule for Leadership Development." CCL, December 14, 2022. https://www.ccl.org/articles/leading-effectively-articles/70-20-10-rule/.

[19] Newkirk, Pamela, Diversity Inc.: The Failed Promise of a Billion-Dollar Business. (2019)

promoting accountability, they engage members who might have previously been cool to diversity projects and increase contact among the women, minorities, and white men that participate..."

DEI training as we know it was built to fail. Many companies want to maintain the status quo while marketing themselves as being serious about creating change, and that's why they like to reach out to DEI practitioners only for the one-day trainings, not ongoing development. Executives and DEI Leaders have to acknowledge doing the same old unconscious bias training isn't going to work. Continuing to do the same thing and hoping for different results is not only the definition of insanity but also a quick way for your organization to waste millions of dollars in training, burn out your leaders, and weaken the credibility of the diversity and inclusion industry. If training is part of your strategy to address anti-Black racism in the workplace, it should be used to introduce the systemic changes and support long-term personal and professional leadership development. Development has to be re-imagined beyond the workshop training model. We have to be ready to try some new tools instead of searching for more hammers.

Questions for Reflection

1. If you were the District Director or Executive at Starbucks, what would you have done differently?

2. Have you attended any corporate DEI training? What was your experience?

3. How did it change you, your team, or the organization?

4. If you could switch the current DEI trainings to a meaningful Personal & Professional Development program, what would you do differently? What would you Start, Stop, and Continue?

Chapter 3

Black Representation

Part 1: Power and Cultural Change

Lack of Black representation is the symptom of anti-Black racism, not the root cause.

In 2018, the retail giant, H&M, released an ad with a Black boy modeling the "Coolest Monkey in the Jungle" sweatshirt. Immediately, we heard an uproar from all over the world. We saw social media statements like, "If there was a Black person in the room, this would have never happened." The common assumption is that there is no way this would have happened if the organization had a diverse Board of Directors, Executive Leadership Team, and marketing team. However, this isn't always the case. Sometimes, there is a Black person in the room who isn't willing to speak up or doesn't even have the authority to do so. Stopping at just adding Black representation isn't enough to prevent these incidences.

H&M responded by hiring Ezinne Okoro, a Black woman, as the North American Head of Diversity & Inclusion the same year as the controversy and backlash. Fortunately, in the case of H&M,

Okoro was able to make some meaningful systemic changes in her short two years with the company, which we will discuss later in this chapter.[20]

My primary concern is that most organizations will stop their anti-racism efforts at "representation numbers" while never challenging structural racism. Representation alone doesn't change the company culture or the systems in place that support structural racism. It only results in a higher percentage of Black people experiencing a toxic work environment.

Chasing the Diversity Numbers

The diversity numbers game isn't a very effective strategy for improving the system because historically, it hasn't worked. Companies have been chasing the numbers for close to 50 years, and it has been like playing a game of whack-a-mole throughout their organizations. They fix one department, and as soon as they hop to the next issue or department, the representation numbers fall again. Even those making a genuine, dedicated effort, slide right back to low representation numbers across the company or in the specific departments of focus.

For example, after Coca-Cola's $192.5 million race-discrimination class-action lawsuit in 2000, they vowed to become the "gold standard" of fairness. In their efforts to improve Black

---

[20] Asare, Janice Gassam. "How H&M Has Completely Revamped Their Diversity And Inclusion Training." Forbes, March 18, 2020.
https://www.forbes.com/sites/janicegassam/2020/03/18/how-hm-has-completely-revamped-their-diversity-and-inclusion-training/?sh=5ac099fa5df0.

representation, they increased from 1.5% Black executives to 15% by 2010. In 2020, Black executive representation went back down to 8%, and their full staff is at 15% (5% lower than 2000).[21] An increase in representation isn't sustainable without systemic change. Instead, I suggest that CEOs focus on removing the systemic barriers that are impeding representation. Systemic change is the action, and representation is the result. Not vice versa. You have to find the cause and cure the disease, not the symptom. What is the root cause of your company's lack of racial diversity, more specifically, the lack of Black employees?

Another reason we shouldn't focus solely on the Black representation numbers as the primary solution to stop acts of racism is because some of the organizations making the mistakes actually have Black representation. The questions we haven't asked are if they have the authority to speak up, and if they spoke up, would anyone listen? According to Connie Wang, the author of the article "The Real Story Behind H&M's Racist Monkey Sweatshirt", H&M's primary issue wasn't Black representation. Wang's theory is that it was more related to culture and process. The H&M Stockholm location and the photo studio had Black employees. However, before the incident there wasn't an opportunity for employees to flag garments at every

---

[21] Maloney, Jennifer, and Lauren Weber. "Coke's Elusive Goal: Boosting Its Black Employees." *WSJ*, December 16, 2020. https://www.wsj.com/articles/coke-resets-goal-of-boosting-black-employees-after-20-year-effort-loses-ground-11608139999.

stage of the process. There was only one person doing the flagging, and now there are five.[22]

When a company improves in representation without making any improvements to the system, it is likely it will only be a temporary gain. We need to shoot for sustainability. The H&M incident happened in Stockholm but it negatively impacted H&M stores in the U.S. and across the globe. Let this be a lesson to global organizations that if addressing racism isn't part of the global diversity discussion, it will wind up back on your U.S. doorstep.

Black Representation with Power and Influence

Putting "Black faces in high places" is a common strategy when companies are riddled in controversy. Also known as tokenism. This is when companies hire or promote a Black person into a high visibility, senior leadership role to calm down the tensions after a racist act, while at the same time keeping the status quo. It's such a common practice it's hard to tell when the intentions are genuine. Thankfully, at H&M and the Washington Football organization, we have seen good examples of positive changes implemented by newly appointed Black leaders in power.

At the start of the 2020 National Football League season, Jason Wright was named the new president of the Washington Football team, making him the first Black team president in the NFL. He took the helm of an organization with 87 years of using a racial slur as their

---

[22] Wang, Connie. "The Real Story Behind H&M's Racist Monkey Sweatshirt." Refinery29, July 11, 2019. https://www.refinery29.com/en-us/2019/07/237347/h-m-racist-hoodie-controversy-diversity-problem.

team's name and an owner, Dan Snyder, who vowed never to change the name despite the outcries. The Washington Football team is also known for being the last NFL team to integrate in 1962. With the checkered history of the team and owner, many people asked if this was another case of a "Black face in a high place".

During this heightened awareness around social justice and the ease with which negative news spreads on social media, companies are learning that people will check back in to see if any real action has been taken. If you don't show meaningful results, it will be called out as window dressing. Thankfully, Jason Wright stepped in and brought visible results immediately. Removing the offensive team name was a good sign that this was a genuine move toward real change. When Wright was questioned about his race playing a role in being selected for the position, his response was perfect, "The fact that I happen to be Black and the most qualified person for this is a boost." It appears Dan Synder finally came to the conclusion that racism is bad for business. Wright was the boost the Washington Football team desperately needed.

H&M also found Black leadership. In January 2018, H&M appointed its first-ever Global Head of Inclusion & Diversity, Annie Wu, who then hired Erinn Okoro, a Black woman, as the North American Head of Inclusion & Diversity later in the year. With the leadership of Okoro and Wu, they took H&M's diversity strategy beyond just hiring and promoting two People of Color, and change processes. This included:

- New opportunities to flag garments and makes notes about particular sensitivities at every step of their 7-step processing system for all new clothing
- A system where at least 12 people in the studio see a photo after it is uploaded
- Increasing the final round of quality checks from one to five

They are hoping these systemic changes result in a change in the culture and the employees' perception of H&M, which will be measured on their employee engagement surveys[23][24].

Black executives taking high profile roles during turmoil must provide clear, specific statements on precisely what will change and have some early big wins like Jason Wright and Erin Okoro. If you're only highlighting the new Black face and making a vague statement about your commitment to improving racial diversity, your company is heading down the road of window dressing.

Dig Deeper: Cultural Change Is a Long Game

I spoke with Nathaniel "Nat" Alston, Jr., President & Founder of The Horizon Group, a human capital consulting firm specializing in human resource strategic planning, talent acquisition, management development training, and succession planning. Nat is also the founder and chairman of the National Association of African-

---

[23] WPSU - Penn State Public Media. https://www.pagecentertraining.psu.edu/public-relations-ethics/introduction-to-diversity-and-public-relations/lesson-2-how-to-reach-diverse-stakeholders/reaching-diverse-stakeholders-externally/.
[24] Wang, Connie. "The Real Story Behind H&M's Racist Monkey Sweatshirt." Refinery29, July 11, 2019. https://www.refinery29.com/en-us/2019/07/237347/h-m-racist-hoodie-controversy-diversity-problem.

Americans in Human Resources (NAAAHR). When asked about his thoughts on Black representation in corporate America, Nat explained how much more work needs to be done:

> *Corporate America still doesn't get it. They are still checking the box. Just look at their Board of Directors. NAAAHR is bombarded with requests for partnerships and unconscious bias training. They want the affiliation, partnership, and training for the optics. Most don't have Black representation that has budget authority, or influence over the hiring above and below. We have to dive deep to change a culture, it's a long game. Cultural change takes 5-7 years. I recommend for corporations that are serious about representation to put Black people on their Board of Directors and to recruit at the high levels, not just the low-level jobs. Companies need to stop the lip service, photo ops, box-checking, and the hiring of D&I officers with no power and authority. They have to go beyond sending funds to HBCUs (Historically Black Colleges & Universities) and begin developing long-term, sustainable relationships. Companies need to build internship programs, do business with HBCUs, and put HBCU presidents on their Boards.*

As Nat shared, companies have the opportunity to build deeper, long-term, relationships with HBCUs when they go beyond the financial gifts. In July 2021, Vanguard Group, the investment management giant, added David A. Thomas, the president of the HBCU, Morehouse College. Thomas is also the co-author of *Breaking Through: The Making of Minority Executives in Corporate America*, and has decades of experience consulting companies on D&I and organizational change. Vanguard Group expanded their board of director seats from 10 to 11 in order to add their 2nd Black director, Thomas, after joining The Board Challenge in 2020. The Philadelphia Business Journal explained, "Last September, more than 40 companies joined The Board Challenge, a movement to improve the representation of Black directors in the boardrooms of the U.S. public and private companies. Pledge and charter partners and supporters were asked to add one Black board member within a year's time and introduce the concept to their networks." [25] [26] This board addition built a bridge to a long-term partnership between Vanguard Group and Morehouse College, and in the long run should equate to Vanguard Group gaining more Black high-income clients, and a stronger Black employee pipeline.

The opportunities to build meaningful relationships are available. Companies shouldn't have a hard time finding the Black talent needed for their boards. They didn't have any trouble finding the Black talent to speak at their town halls and community listening session in 2020 during and after the protests.

---

[25] **Blumenthal, Jeff. "Vanguard adds college president as second Black board member."** Philadelphia Business Journal July 23, 2021.
https://www.bizjournals.com/philadelphia/news/2021/07/23/vanguard-adds-morehouse-college-president-as-secon.html

[26] "The Board Challenge – Supporting Diversity on Your Board of Directors," n.d. https://theboardchallenge.org/.

Setting Black Representation Targets

A long list of companies made pledges in 2020. Many organizations specifically said they were going to make improvements within their own company regarding Black Representation (The Aspen Digital Anti-Racism Pledge Tracker – The Aspen Institute)[27]:

- **Dell Technologies** committed to the goal of achieving 25% of its U.S. workforce, and 15% of its U.S. leadership, comprising people who are Black/African-American and Hispanic/Latinx.

- **Facebook** is committing to having 30% more people of color, including 30% more Black people, in leadership positions by 2025.

- **H.P.** has pledged to double its number of Black and African-American executives by 2025.

- **Microsoft** pledged to double the number of Black and African-American managers, senior individual contributors, and senior leaders at its company in the U.S. by 2025.

- **Uber** plans to double Black representation in its leadership roles (i.e., Director titles and above) by 2025 through pipeline development and hiring.

---

[27] Aspen Institute. "The Aspen Digital Anti-Racism Pledge Tracker". June 25, 2020 https://www.aspeninstitute.org/blog-posts/aspen-digital-anti-racism-pledge-tracker/

These organizations were specific about their aim to address the needs of Black/African-American representation instead of hiding behind the vagueness of "People of Color" or "underrepresented groups". However, the most transparent way to share your target goals would be to state your current representation numbers. For example, we don't know how many Black executives H.P. has at their organization. If they only have 2 Black executives, doubling the Black executive representation by 2025 wouldn't be a very bold goal. Also, if they reached their goal by 2025 to double the number of Black/African-American executives, what percentage of the total executives would be Black? These are the answers that employees working to make improvements to achieve these commitments want to know. If you don't know what "double" means, how would you know if you are on target? Employees are volunteering on the internal virtual conference, sitting in focus groups, taking surveys, and leading business resource groups, but they don't have any clarity on the target. Quite often this data is only shared in an executive committee and in small human resource pockets. Employees at all levels are lost and will not know if their efforts are helpful until January 2025, when it's too late. Maybe H.P. has shared this information internally, but most companies don't.

For all organizations, large and small, your transparency will be graded by those paying attention inside and outside your organization. The Aspen Institution is one of many great resources for tracking these promises. We will see who hits their 2025 targets, and who just gave lip service, or failed due to a weak strategy.

Avoiding Racial Preference

Setting targets for Black representation has become an area of concern again. Leaders have to be careful about the specific tactics implemented to achieve the goal of racial equity in the workplace. Those big headlines about your organization addressing racial justice inside and outside the company may have stopped the community from protesting against you in the street and on social media, but as you should know, not every group is interested in stopping anti-Black racism in the workplace.

In 2020, Microsoft's pledged to increase Black representation drew the attention of the Labor Department's Office of Federal Contract Compliance Programs. The Labor Department immediately began an investigation of Microsoft to determine whether they were violating the Civil Rights Act by setting targets to increase Black representation. Craig Leen, director of the Labor Department's Office of Federal Contract Compliance Program stated, "Although contractors must establish affirmative action programs to set workforce utilization goals for minorities and women based on availability, contractors must not engage in discriminatory practices in meeting those goals."[28] Coming under fire when you commit to improving Black representation should not worry you if your action plan is "system" focused. The Labor Department appreciated that

---

[28] Guynn, Jessica Usa Today. "Microsoft Plan to Increase Black Representation in Its U.S. Workforce Probed by Labor Department." USA TODAY, October 7, 2020. https://eu.usatoday.com/story/tech/2020/10/06/microsoft-diversity-african-americans-black-department-of-labor-trump-george-floyd/5902478002/.

Microsoft stated they are not engaging in racial preference (hiring based solely on race) in their outreach goals.

Setting Black representation targets is a good thing. The critical part is how they will be achieved. Will it be by removing the barriers within your organization that have caused Black employees to leave, not be promoted, hired, or even attracted to your brand, or are you practicing racial preferences, aka quotas, during hiring? If it is everything mentioned other than "racial preference," you are on the path of sustainable change to reduce discrimination against Black people and improve the representation. If it's "racial preference", you will only have a short-lived boost in representation, if any, and may face legal troubles.

Try this self-assessment. Did you start with reviewing the company's racial demographic data? Is the problem due to practices and policies related to recruiting, hiring, onboarding, or retention? Has your outreach ever included advertising opportunities through Black Media outlets, Black Associations, or Historically Black Colleges and Universities?

You Don't Have to Sacrifice Fairness and Quality

Another mistake organizations make while addressing Black representation is underestimating concerns about merit, fairness, quality of hires, and standards within the organization. When implementing strategies to dismantle anti-Black racism at the individual, group, and system levels, all colleagues need to be reassured that the company is not sacrificing its integrity in the process.

Robert Livingston, the author of "The Conversation: How Seeking and Speaking the Truth About Racism Can Radically Transform Individuals and Organizations", addresses this executive concern in his Harvard Business Review article, Livingston says:

> "The assumptions of sacrifice have enormous implications for the hiring and promotion of diverse talent, for at least two reasons. First, people often assume that increasing diversity means sacrificing principles of fairness and merit and because it requires giving "special" favors to people of color rather than treating everyone the same." He goes on to share, "The second assumption many people have is that increasing diversity requires sacrificing high quality and standards." [29]

Many leaders often hesitate to act on diversity goals because they worry about sacrificing their principles of fairness and quality. When employees assume that in order to increase Black representation, they have to hire a less talented person, it is detrimental to the organization. This belief could result in a toxic work environment for the newly hired or promoted person. What a horrible start for the incoming leaders to join a company with no trust or support from the team! Not to mention, this thinking is also a key

---

[29] Harvard Business Review. "How to Promote Racial Equity in the Workplace," November 10, 2020. https://hbr.org/2020/09/how-to-promote-racial-equity-in-the-workplace).

reason why other colleagues could feel slighted. And when a "diverse" hire doesn't work, we wonder why it wasn't successful.

This horrible myth that diverse talent means lesser talent must be dispelled through education and transparency. Communicate the following to your employees:

- Qualifications required for the positions you are hiring for
- Hiring and promotion standards and procedures
- How past mistakes of your company impacted your current lack of representation
- How you have taken responsibility for the company's past transgressions of racism and discrimination against Black people
- How you aim to remedy the inequality you have caused in Black employees and community members

Transparency and education are crucial to dispelling this myth. Ignoring or underestimating these assumptions and concerns could be a costly mistake. Instead, meet it head on.

The Gender Representation Movement Is Not the Same Model

Although companies have a long way to go in achieving full gender equity, they have made more progress in the advancement for white women than any other protected demographic since the Civil Rights Act of 1964. Time Magazine's 2013 article, "Affirmative Action Has Helped White Women More Than Anyone", by Sally Kohn, points to multiple studies showing the disparity in progress since affirmative action.[30] LeanIn.org and McKinsey's Women in the Workplace 2016 study, shared that women make up 19% of the C-suite, 33% directors, 24% senior vice presidents, and 37% managerial positions. The Women in the Workplace article also states, "Today (2020), 44 percent of companies have three or more women in their C-suite, up from 29 percent of companies in 2015."[31] And at the same time Black professionals in 2018 held just 3.3% of all executive or senior leadership roles.[32] In June 2020, out of the Fortune 500 organizations, there are 38 female CEOs, while only three are women of color, and less than 1% of the Fortune 500 CEOs are Black People. That's four Black people.[33] There is clearly a disparity between the progress of gender diversity and racial diversity in the corporate America. Why is this the case?

The Society of Human Resource Management (SHRM) found an essential piece of the puzzle – cultural norms. SHRM says the focus of diversity efforts in most parts of the world is on hiring and promoting women. The SHRM's Diversity & Inclusion study states,

---

[30] Kohn, Sally. "Affirmative Action Has Helped White Women More Than Anyone." Time, June 17, 2013. https://time.com/4884132/affirmative-action-civil-rights-white-women/.
[31] McKinsey & Company. "Women in the Workplace 2022," October 18, 2022. https://www.mckinsey.com/featured-insights/diversity-and-inclusion/women-in-the-workplace.
[32] Sahadi, Jeanne. "After Years of Talking about Diversity, the Number of Black Leaders at US Companies Is Still Dismal." CNN, June 2, 2020. https://edition.cnn.com/2020/06/02/success/diversity-and-black-leadership-in-corporate-america/index.html.
[33] Benveniste, Alexis. "The Fortune 500 Now Has a Record Number of Female CEOs: A Whopping 38." CNN, August 4, 2020. https://edition.cnn.com/2020/08/04/business/fortune-500-women-ceos/index.html.

"Women are also comparatively easy to integrate into organizations since – gender issues aside – they typically have grown up in the same country as their male colleagues, and hence tend to share the prevailing cultural norms."[34] During affirmative action, minorities and women were being integrated into corporations that were all predominately white males. White males already interacted with white women outside of work. Most white men have a white mother, aunt, sister, wife, cousins, daughter, and friends. The cultural norms are similar and comfortable.

Most global companies are more likely to prioritize an issue that is relevant everywhere. For example, there may not be much racial or ethnic diversity to manage in a city like Bozeman, Montana that is 90% white, but no matter where you are in the U.S., there will be gender diversity to measure and manage. In addition, most CEOs could connect to this gender diversity because they directly experience it in their life. They already have relationships with women and shared cultural norms. It becomes the diversity path of least resistance in the workplace. As a result, gender diversity has been prioritized over racial diversity and this is a key reason why gender diversity has been more successful.

---

[34] Society for Human Resource Management: Global Diversity and Inclusion: Perceptions, Practices and Attitudes. 2009. Page 9

Even Sheryl Sandberg recognizes this in her Wall Street Journal article:

> "More companies prioritize gender diversity than racial diversity, perhaps hoping that focusing on gender alone will be sufficient to support all women. But women of color face bias both for being women and for being people of color, and this double discrimination leads to a complex set of constraints and barriers."[35]

Racial diversity has not been prioritized, and specifically Black representation has been outright ignored. The topic of improving racial equity has been taboo and a much more uncomfortable conversation than other diversity issues. I was hoping to find a special initiative that helped reduce the barriers of representation of women that we could leverage for racial diversity efforts, but it seems to be pointing only to the "desire for change". A company has to have the desire to put in the hard work of implementing and maintaining initiatives to improve Black representation.[36]

---

[35] Sandberg, Sheryl, and Rachel Thomas. "Sheryl Sandberg on How to Get to Gender Equality." WSJ, October 10, 2017. https://www.wsj.com/articles/sheryl-sandberg-on-how-to-get-to-gender-equality-1507608721.
[36] Council, Forbes Coaches. "13 Ideas To Promote Female Equality In The Workplace." Forbes, April 8, 2016.
https://www.forbes.com/sites/forbescoachescouncil/2016/04/08/13-ideas-to-promote-female-equality-in-the-workplace/?sh=7c54d77e3f14.

Questions for Reflection

1. How did you feel when you heard about H&M's "coolest monkey in the jungle" sweatshirt?

2. How successful have your efforts been to improve the Black representation of your organization?

3. Who has the power and influence? Who has budget authority and influence over hiring decisions above and below?

4. Has your company set targets for Black employee representation? What are the current numbers?

5. Besides "racial preference", are there any other legal concerns to be aware of when setting representation targets.

Part 2: The Talent Pipeline Myth

"Corporate heads shouldn't blame a limited pool of talent on their inability to promote and hire Black executives"

— **Kenneth Chenault, the former CEO of American Express Co**

Recruit: Don't Blame the Talent Pipeline

The Talent Pipeline Myth: There aren't enough Black people gaining the skills and knowledge required for the position, but when they acquire the proper knowledge and skills, they will have a fair opportunity to be hired. Only then will companies begin increasing the Black representation at their organization. Ultimately, it's not me (the company), it's you (lack of talented Black people).

In corporate America, the talent pipeline means the number of qualified candidates available for a given role. Since integrating the workplace in the '60s, the lack of talented Black people available for the positions has been the primary excuse for the slow progress in improving Black representation. However, decades later, leaders continue to have low Black representation and are still blaming the talent pipeline. Kenneth Chenault says in the Bloomberg news article:

> "While "it's a cop-out" to blame the talent pipeline, there are some areas where there are issues of supply, but I think there are many areas where the talent is there. In some areas, getting a few diverse

people in position, what you see over time is that leads to an increase more broadly in diversity across the company."[37]

There may be some specialty areas where fewer Black candidates are available, but this does not explain the low representation across industries and levels. Corporate leaders must begin taking responsibility for their company's numbers and stop using the tired excuse "it's not us, it's a pipeline problem."

The Tech industry's talent pipeline has been a heated discussion for several years. Like many other sectors, the tech sector acknowledges the lack of representation and expresses the desire to do better but has not made much progress. In a 2016 NPR article, Facebook said representation in technology or any other industry would depend upon more people having the opportunity to gain necessary skills through public education.[38] In other words, they doubled down on the lack of Black talent narrative by blaming the quality of public education.

The lack of an educated talent pool is not a reasonable answer to this issue. According to a USA Today analysis in 2014, they found that top universities turn out Black and Hispanic computer science

---

[37] Square, Jennifer. "CEOs Lamenting Diversity Pipeline Is a 'Cop-Out,' Chenault Says" Bloomberg.com, December 8, 2020
"https://www.bloomberg.com/news/articles/2020-12-08/ceos-lamenting-diversity-pipeline-is-a-cop-out-chenault-says

[38] Selyukh, Alina. "Why Some Diversity Thinkers Aren't Buying The Tech Industry's Excuses." NPR.org, July 19, 2016.
https://www.npr.org/sections/alltechconsidered/2016/07/19/486511816/why-some-diversity-thinkers-arent-buying-the-tech-industrys-excuses.

and computer engineering graduates at twice the rate the leading technology companies hire them.[39]

The second excuse Facebook gave was that tech jobs are just a different beast, and should not get the same scrutiny as other industries. Another weak reason because tech companies have a tough time explaining the talent pipeline issue for even their non-tech positions.[40] If the low Black representation is solely based on specific tech skills, then why do these same tech companies typically lack Black representation in human resources, marketing, communications, accounting, legal and other departments?

The Talent Pipeline Myth Is Coming Undone

A company's image plays a major factor in the ability to recruit Black talent. The quickest way to chase Black talent away is to make disparaging remakes about their community's talent. Comments insinuating that Black talent means inferior talent are based on white supremacist thinking and should be challenged immediately. The CEO of Wells Fargo, Charles Scharf, blamed the pipeline in 2020 by saying, "While it might sound like an excuse, the unfortunate reality is that there is a very limited pool of Black talent to recruit from with

---

[39] Guynn, Elizabeth Usa Weise And Jessica Today. "Black and Hispanic Computer Scientists Have Degrees from Top Universities, but Don't Get Hired in Tech." USA TODAY, July 20, 2020. https://eu.usatoday.com/story/tech/2014/10/12/silicon-valley-diversity-tech-hiring-computer-science-graduates-african-american-hispanic/14684211/.

[40] Selyukh, Alina. "Why Some Diversity Thinkers Aren't Buying The Tech Industry's Excuses." NPR.org, July 19, 2016.
https://www.npr.org/sections/alltechconsidered/2016/07/19/486511816/why-some-diversity-thinkers-arent-buying-the-tech-industrys-excuses.

this specific experience as our industry does not have enough diversity in most senior roles."[41]

Scharf rightfully received a great deal of backlash. So much that soon after, he had to issue an apology for the statement. Making comments like this have a long-term impact on the company's reputation, brand and the performance of recruiters. It's hard for the recruiter to bring in Black talent when the CEO is implying that there is no reason to look there because that racial group has less talent than other racial groups. Even after the apology, the Wells Fargo recruiters and other leaders already have a built-in excuse ready if Black representation remains low. They could always refer back to the CEO's comment that it is a very limited pool of talent. The corporate promises and pledges to increase Black representation will not mean much if they have a ready-made excuse for not meeting their 2025 goals.

What is the current state of the corporate pipeline, and how are companies doing in their effort to improve Black representation? According to the 2019 study conducted by the National Opinion Research Center and the Center for Talent Innovation, corporate America isn't doing too well: [42]

---

[41] Yahoo.com. https://finance.yahoo.com/news/wells-fargo-ceo-remarks-show-mindset-that-sees-black-worker-training-as-charity-operation-191412215.html.
[42] Bunn, Curtis. "Blacks in Corporate America Still Largely Invisible, Study Finds." NBC News, December 11, 2019. https://www.nbcnews.com/news/nbcblk/blacks-corporate-america-still-largely-invisible-study-finds-n1098981.

- ☼ While African Americans make up 10 percent of college graduates, there are only four black CEOs at Fortune 500 companies.

- ☼ Only 3.2 percent of executives and senior manager-level employees are African American.

- ☼ 38% percent of Black millennials say they are considering leaving their jobs to start their own company.

- ☼ Large companies are likely to reflect the systemic racism of American society due to their size and age. In contrast, smaller companies are more likely to be counter-cultural, which is a threat to the future success of large companies.

Due to these headwinds Black employees face when advancing within the corporate structure, more Black employees are beginning to look for alternative opportunities as entrepreneurs and joining medium and small start-up companies. This trend will continue if large Fortune 500 companies continue to deny their role in creating an environment that has blocked Black talent from the opportunity to join their company and advance.

It is a repetitive cycle. First, there is low Black representation at most organizations, and the percentage continues to decrease at higher levels of position. Secondly, companies acknowledge this disparity and state that they desire to do better. And lastly, when organizations don't achieve any improvements in Black representation, they say their failure to make improvements is due to the lack of Black people with the knowledge and skills to do the job – the talent pipeline.

The "Lack of Black People in the Talent Pipeline" is a Myth. There are over 50,000 Black students who graduate from Historically Black Colleges and Universities every year, which accounts for only 20% of the Black college graduates.[43] There is plenty of talent available at all levels, from entry-level to the executive level, and across industries. When this myth is recognized for what it is— a very dangerous myth— leaders could begin learning why their company's talent pipeline is the problem, and ultimately identify and correct the systemic barriers that cause their company to miss the mark.

What's the Real Reason Your Pipeline Lacks Black Talent?

The truth is not everyone will be an A-level candidate, regardless of race. When the candidate is Black, it shouldn't be limited to the super-talented Barack and Michelles of the world or the Ivy League graduates that exceed all of the preferred job requirements. It is not a fair expectation to ask all Black candidates to be a sure bet. Do we ask for all of the white candidates to be overqualified or are we hiring on potential? At all organizations, talent varies from the exceptional down to the total bust. If you're only willing to hire the perfect Black employee, why aren't all of your other employees perfect?

---

[43] United Negro College Fund. "HBCU Economic Impact Report." UNCF, June 16, 2021. https://uncf.org/programs/hbcu-impact.

Matthew Spencer, the CEO of an AI-driven hiring tool, also supports the idea of exploring Black talent beyond the Ivy League graduates. He explained that prestige doesn't result in high potential employees. Spencer says, "Prestige, however, does not equate to potential. But these shortcuts are straightforward, safe, and before the invention of things like artificial intelligence, even understandable …we have watched our A.I. software champion for five times more highly qualified candidates who are people of color, and five times more highly qualified "non-target" school candidates, than what firms would normally be directly exposed to in their processes. It's simply a matter of believing that there are highly qualified candidates at every school, and bringing their resumes to the top of the stack."[44]

If A.I. evidence isn't compelling enough to make you rethink the universities or associations you target, maybe the success of Vice President of the United States of America, Kamala Harris, caught your attention. She graduated from Howard University, a Historically Black College and University (HBCU), and is a member of a Black sorority, Alpha Kappa Alpha Inc. Businesses must begin to realize there is plenty of talent at HBCUs. If you don't rethink your recruiting process and how you view the non-target schools, your organization will not achieve the new representation numbers they promised to accomplish.

---

[44] "Fastcompany.Com," n.d. https://www.fastcompany.com/90561692/dont-blame-your-lack-of-diversity-on-the-pipeline-blame-your-process.

The term "Executive Presence" is another reason your pipeline isn't diverse. One of the common barriers that get in the way of creating a racially diverse talent pipeline at the senior level is the myth of Executive Presence. This term is just as vague as "cultural fit". Ask ten people what executive presence means, and you will probably get ten different answers. Everyone is on the mythical quest to find this special, unique, innate leadership presence in themselves and others. Regardless of how people define this, it has resulted in the hiring of mostly white men over 6 feet tall. In some cases, it is the Warren Harding Effect that Malcolm Gladwell shared in his book, *Blink*. While the average height of men in the U.S. is 5'9", the average CEO is over 6 feet tall. [45] It is fair to say executive presence has been heavily weighted in appearance. If executive presence isn't about height, it is gender and race, or the quality of their suit, shoes, type of hairstyle, etc., when it should be defined by behavior, emotional intelligence, talent, and knowledge.

Talent assessments could help reduce some biases when considering an executive role. The Gallup Organization identified five key dimensions of Executive Talent – Direction, Drive, Influence, Relationships, and Execution, and has built an assessment to better measure these talent dimensions. Whether you're working with Gallup or another management consulting firm, it is critical to prevent your organization from falling for the same mistake of only hiring and promoting people to executive-level positions because they

---

[45] Gladwell, Malcolm, Blink: The Powe of Thinking Without Thinking (New York, NY, 2005)

mirror most CEOs' looks. It is essential to get past the looks and the charm and not fall for the old, archaic ideas of executive presence, and instead identify a more objective approach to your talent assessment.

The third reason there is a lack of Black diversity in the pipeline is poor sourcing and recruiting. For those interested in sourcing and recruiting Black talent, the formula is relatively easy to follow. This is how companies found me after undergraduate and graduate school:

My undergraduate degree was in Hospitality & Tourism: Business Administration. The founder of this new School of Business program, Dr. Beverly Bryant, had great relationships with companies throughout Raleigh/Durham, North Carolina. Thanks to Dr. Bryant's connections, I was able the do internships at the Sheraton Imperial Hotel and a Durham Country Club. Upon graduating, I joined the Darden Restaurant Management Training Program. Darden, the Sheraton, and the country club all had a critical thing in common; they all decided to build a relationship with a Historically Black College & University, my alma mater, North Carolina Central University. It is that simple. It doesn't take rocket science to find Black talent. In addition to this, our Hospitality program was a member of the National Society of Minorities in Hospitality. This association, NSMH, is a non-profit organization founded to educate, encourage, and empower minority students interested in pursuing hospitality careers. They had regional and national conferences and provided opportunities for organizations to interview and recruit students from HBCUs.

Years later, after earning my master's degree in Organizational Psychology, I connected with The Gallup Organization. I met them at a career fair held at the Thurgood Marshall College Fund Leadership Conference in New York City. It's an annual four-day conference intended to develop students' leadership skills, create a community of scholars, provide companies access to a talented and diverse student population, and help students make connections that lead to careers.[46]

Companies that are intentionally looking to build a diverse talent pipeline with Black candidates know there are over 100 HBCUs to recruit from, as well as Black-focused associations for almost every industry. For those that say they can't find Black talent, even those looking for engineers, I really wonder how they can't. When I speak to leaders that say they can't find Black engineers, I usually ask if they ever heard of the North Carolina A&T University or the National Society of Black Engineers. The talent is there and available at these locations and beyond.

Bold Strategies to Improve the Pipeline

One of the key components to sourcing talent is the company's image. The question may be, "what has your company done to lose the respect and trust of the Black community?" Company image matters to candidates. It is vital to know your company's history and take the time to "right the wrongs". If not, your attempts to reach out to an HBCU or directly to a Black senior leader could seem

---

[46] Thurgood Marshall College Fund. "22nd Annual Leadership Institute," August 17, 2022. https://www.tmcf.org/students-alumni/22nd-annual-leadership-institute/.

disingenuous. If your company has a poor reputation, you may want to start by implementing anti-racism policies and practice within your company and correct past mistakes. Which could include making sure your job descriptions focus on potential over credentials, using a diverse interview panel, and linking your Black representation number to executive-level compensation.[47]

One of the most important items for organizations to consider is implementing a special program dedicated specifically to building the Black talent pipeline. Executives and D&I leaders talk about reforming their current talent pipeline programs to include more Black people, but they stop short of dedicating a special program to address the Black talent pipeline issue specifically. Special programs are needed to remedy past wrongs from organizations and society, but they often hesitate when it comes to building specific programs for Black talent because they are worried about it being perceived as special treatment.

JPMorgan Chase is one of the few who weren't afraid to create a program to improve their Black talent pipeline. In 2016 they launched the Advancing Black Pathways (ABP) program, a diversity strategy aimed at attracting, hiring, retaining, and advancing Black talent. Paul Ingram highlighted this ABP program in the Harvard Business Review article titled "The Forgotten Dimensions of

---

[47] "Building a Diverse Talent Pipeline: 6 Meaningful Steps Every Company Can Take," n.d. https://business.linkedin.com/talent-solutions/blog/diversity/2020/building-a-diverse-talent-pipeline.

Diversity."⁴⁸ Ingram explains, "The most effective recruitment programs focus on race and social class simultaneously. That's what JPMorgan Chase does in its Advancing Black Pathways (ABP) program, which gives special attention to first-generation and low-income students in the recruiting it does at HBCUs – an approach it calls recruiting for "diversity within diversity." ABP also supports a financial hardship fund for students at HBCUs, providing money for transportation, technology, and food. The goal is to enable students under financial duress to stay in school and earn their degrees. After participants in the program graduate, ABP maintains contact with them and invites them to apply for internships and jobs."⁴⁹

I spoke with two students that participate in this program. One student is currently in the ABP program and the other student completed the program last year and was invited back as an intern this summer. Both students are having a great experience and are gaining valuable skills and knowledge they could use in the future at JPMorgan Chase or another great company.

The young lady in the ABP program told me it has been inspiring. She also shared that people leading the program and speakers were personable, most of them look like her, and that there were so many executives present and available. The ABP program is for rising juniors. Almost all of these students will be invited for an internship next summer as a rising seniors. The second lady I

---

⁴⁸ Harvard Business Review. "The Forgotten Dimension of Diversity," December 15, 2020. https://hbr.org/2021/01/the-forgotten-dimension-of-diversity.
⁴⁹ Harvard Business Review. "The Forgotten Dimension of Diversity," December 15, 2020. https://hbr.org/2021/01/the-forgotten-dimension-of-diversity.

interviewed is a rising senior, interning in Corporate Client Banking. She shared how much she has enjoyed the sense a Black community that JP Morgan Chase has provided to her in the ABP program and as an intern. She explained that they provide opportunities to connect with other ABP Alumni, the Black Business Resource Group, and allies outside of the Black community. I'm happy to learn that what has been promoted on the ABP marketing page really matched these students' experiences. This is a Black talent recruitment model that could be replicated at other companies.

Those ready to take the next step of implementing policies and programs to address anti-Black racism have to consider creating unique programs that directly address the structural racism of America. JP Morgan Chase's program launched a few years before the Anti-Black Racism awakening of 2020. How many other companies have the courage to do the same?

Recruiting Trends

I had a discussion with Louis Montgomery Jr., who leads JM Search's Human Resources and Diversity Officer Executive Search Practice. Louis has over 25 years of experience as a Human Resource Practitioner and Diversity Leader with several Fortune 100 firms, and has authored several thought-leadership articles on DEI. Louis shared his thoughts on the current recruiting trends:

"I ask leaders, 'What do you mean when you say diversity?" I ask them to stop using the word "diversity candidate" and be more specific about what you need. Frequently they mean women, Black people, Latinx, and sometimes Asian. I suggest for colleagues to use the term "underrepresented" instead of diversity candidate because we all represent dimensions of diversity. I have provided training to colleagues on nomenclature to avoid these awkward moments. They want to know the right terms to use. For example, the term "colored people" in the NAACP, National Association for the Advancement of Colored People. This term is outdated. I prefer to use Black because it's more inclusive of other groups beyond just African-American."

Louis also shared some of the biggest changes he has seen since 2020:

- *Frequently, our clients as they engage us, they are asking for a diverse slate of candidates.*

- *DEI inaugural roles were high in 2020 and 2021, but it started to slow down in 2022. There are so many people that recently moved into a new role it's more challenging to recruit experienced DEI leaders.*

- *There are a lot of DEI leadership roles, so candidates can be more discerning and take the time to ask the right questions.*

- *DE&I initiatives and Leaders are very reliant on Senior Leadership support. Sometimes when new leaders arrive in organizations and if they aren't supportive of DE&I, these initiatives are not pursued and the DE&I leaders' role are negatively impacted.*

Seeing these trends highlights the need for leaders in power to embed anti-racism policies and practices so deep into the organization that it would be hard for someone else to step in and undo the work. This is why it is essential to go beyond setting some funds aside to attend career fairs like the Black MBA conference. The budget to attend a conference or career fair could be easily cut off. However, a deeper relationship like having an HBCU president serving on your board, a recruitment program with a specific HBCU, and a visible, Black focused-internship program, will be harder for an organization to quietly end.

Questions for Reflection

1 How did companies find you?

2 How have you found Black talent?

3 What are the other myths that are hurting the Black talent pipeline?

4 What strategies should companies be implementing to improve their pipeline?

5 Review JPMorgan's Advancing Black Pathways website.

6 Name other programs available that focus specifically on recruiting diverse talent.

Chapter 4

Talking About Race at Work

"I don't like that man. I must get to know him better."

— **Abraham Lincoln**

During the Summer 2020 protests, there were plenty of conversations about race relations and the Black experience. These virtual town halls and conferences about racism were happening across local communities, TV, radio, social media, and in the workplace. They were sometimes called "Uncomfortable Conversations". I viewed these workplace town halls with a healthy skepticism, wondering how we're still having the same conversations explaining racism to people, and at the same time asking myself if executives really want to listen or if we are just wasting our time. It certainly gets exhausting, re-educating other communities about systemic racism and anti-Black racism all over again, but what made this 2020 experience unique was that it was taking place at work like never before.

Previously, Companies Discouraged Conversations About Racism

Many companies had policies prohibiting conversations about race, religion, and politics. Even at the companies that didn't have it as policy, it was highly recommended to avoid these polarizing topics. Even as this "bring your authentic self to work" concept began gaining traction through the field of Diversity & Inclusion, most colleagues treaded lightly on these topics. In the very recent past, race and ethnic expression in the workplace didn't go much beyond potluck cultural lunches or talking about holiday celebrations, and music. Most real conversations about racism were only with the few people you trusted. It was a secret, off the record, discussion. Not a town hall.

In my workplace experience, I told people many times I don't discuss race, politics, or religion at work, because that was the rule I was taught at the first company I joined after college. When I was a manager in 2002 at a restaurant chain, a co-manager asked me, "You don't really think racial oppression still exists and Black people are held back by "The Man", do you?! Slavery was over 200 years ago", my reply was, "You know we aren't supposed to talk about race, religion, and politics at work, right?" Considering the rule, I thought that question was a trap. A few years later, during Hurricane Katrina, a different co-manager had disparaging remarks about the tragedy in New Orleans. He said the Black people of New Orleans didn't evacuate because they wanted to stay around to loot. I just waved him away, told him I wasn't going to waste my time explaining, and I redirected the conversation back to our work duties.

I appreciated people sharing their true nature and bringing their authentic selves to work, especially the racists, because there was an advantage in knowing who I was really working with, but it was still tricky to navigate as a young Black professional. Lauren Liswood wrote about the mouse and the elephant metaphor in her book, *The Loudest Duck: Moving Beyond Diversity While Embracing Differences to Achieve Success at Work*. Liswood writes, "The elephant knows almost nothing about the mouse, while the mouse survives by knowing everything about the other. Herein lies the dynamic between the dominant and the non-dominant."[50]

Paying close attention to my white colleagues' words and behaviors was key to my workplace survival in racist environments. I was learning my colleagues and maneuvering as needed. I believed it was essential to my career growth in the corporate world not to engage in those conversations.

Later in my career, I heard fewer ignorant remarks or overtly racist comments at work. Instead, the workplace just ignored race-related events with a deafening silence. When the police murdered Oscar Grant, no one mentioned it at work. It was a nonfactor. In Washington DC, I even looked out the window and watched a protest against the execution of Atlanta's Troy Davis, and then I returned to my desk as if nothing had happened. When the killing of Trayvon

---

[50] Liswood, Lauren, The Loudest Duck: Moving beyond diversity while embracing differences to achieve success at work. (Hoboken, NJ, 2010)

Martin was all over the news, nobody talked about it at work. When George Zimmerman was acquitted, I remember that day feeling as surreal as 9/11. I wanted to talk to someone about it, but I hadn't been at my new job long enough to know who I could trust. In these moments, I could have benefited from a conversation about these race-related issues at work, but I felt unsafe sharing my thoughts.

Feeling Safe Enough to Share Your Thoughts

According to SHRM's summer 2020 article, colleagues still feel unsafe, uncomfortable, and discouraged despite this new push for conversations about race in the workplace.[51] 47% of Black HR professionals report feeling unsafe sharing their perspectives. In contrast, 28 percent of white HR professionals agree.

- 37% of Black and White workers feel uncomfortable engaging in candid conversations about race at work. 38% of all U.S. workers agree.

- 33% of all U.S. workers say their workplace discourages discussion of racial justice issues. 45% of Black workers, 30% of white workers.

- 43% of all US workers think it's inappropriate to discuss race at work, including 38% of Black workers and 42% of white workers.

---

[51] Society of Human Resource Management: Together Forward @Work, "The Journey to Equity and Inclusion". https://togetherforwardatwork.shrm.org/wp-content/uploads/2020/08/20-1412_TFAW_Report_RND7_Pages.pdf

My 2020 experience talking about race at work felt very different. I talked more about my thoughts with people that weren't Black than I would have ever imagined, and I found the conversations to be meaningful. However, my experience may have been unique due to my role and position. Entry level employees may not have had the same experience. Or it could be because people in my field of Corporate Social Responsibility and Diversity & Inclusion are more willing and able to have these conversations. Were the people I work with the exception to the rule or did other people inside and outside of my workplace have the same positive, meaningful, experience having conversations about racism with colleagues? Is it too dangerous to encourage these talks in the workplace?

The Pros and Cons of the Anti-Racism Town Halls in the Workplace

I reached out to Jana Simon, Diversity Equity & Inclusion Director at a New York Law Firm, to learn about her experience leading conversations in 2020. Jana told me:

> *The pandemic made us realize that we can't separate what's happening in society from the workplace anymore, there are blurred lines everywhere, which includes talking about race. At my previous firm we hosted these conversations because the Black community of the firm felt it needed to be addressed and it was the responsibility of the firm to address it. For all town halls, you want to talk about a topic everyone is thinking about.*
>
> *When it comes to the topic of race, everyone is starting at a different point. There are people paying attention that understand equity and inequity in*

society, who understand police brutality against the Black community, and the history of that... And there are people that don't care about this, and wonder why are we talking about it in the workplace, and there were other Black attorneys and staff that felt this is bs, that this is not enough and we don't have to educate white people.

For a lot of Town Halls, the Black community was asked to tell people about their experiences. We wanted to create spaces for members of the Black community to share their experiences, but we didn't want people of color to carry the emotional burden of bringing us all along. You will never get it all right but it's important to talk about it... and whatever your town hall looks like, it has to match your core company values.

Jana highlighted the complexity of trying to host anti-Black racism conversations with people who have a variety of experiences, backgrounds, and opinions about anti-Black racism. As an experienced DEI practitioner, she knew this conversation was necessary because it was on everyone's mind and the community asked for the space.

Many organizations used the town hall format for their conversations about racism with mixed results. The conversation about racism should happen, but the format and how it is facilitated matters. For example, LinkedIn's virtual town hall turned out to be a disaster. It left employees feeling the executive team wasn't taking the issue seriously, and they were also triggered by the anonymous racist comments in the chat box. In respond, an employee commented,

"There are some extremely offensive comments here that go completely against the spirit of what this is intended for. I am COMPLETELY shocked by some of these racist comments from my fellow employees. I am thoroughly disgusted!".[52] It highlighted the need not only to restrict the anonymous comments in a virtual forum but also for leadership to come better prepared. Employees expected the newly appointed CEO, Ryan Roslansky, to say something more meaningful than, "I don't have the answers."

The company-wide town hall format also makes it difficult for everyone to share their experiences and feel heard when attending in person or virtually with thousands of people. Other Diversity, Equity & Inclusion Leaders I interviewed found some success in providing employees with smaller group discussions on race.

Bama Athreya, human rights activist and DEI practitioner, shared, "Our organization added the DEI circles monthly. No more than ten people for 30 minutes long. Not a set topic by month, just what was needed, without a scripted conversation. For example, a conversation starter would be - tell us the first time you had an experience with a Black person, or tell us about a time when you were an active bystander and didn't respond right." These small voluntary group conversations also known as listening circles give colleagues a

---

[52] Business Insider Nederland. "Leaks of 'disturbing' and 'racist' comments from a LinkedIn staff meeting show the challenges facing diversity and inclusion efforts in corporate America," June 8, 2020. https://www.businessinsider.nl/linkedin-racism-work-town-hall-company-culture-diversity-inclusion-2020-6?international=true&r=US.

chance to speak, listen, and feel, and could create mutual understanding and support.

Another DEI training practitioner I spoke to also witnessed some success with facilitating conversations in small groups, but was concerned about its lack of impact company-wide. She said the small groups became an echo chamber, and it didn't change the larger systemic issues at her company.

Conversations about race in the workplace whether company-wide or in small groups is very new to leaders and employees. It's difficult to get it right the first time, but the conversation is necessary. It's not going to be perfect, but in time you will find the format that works best for your corporate culture.

Conversations About Racism Required Courage

Not everyone had the same experience attempting to introduce this "Uncomfortable Conversation" town hall about racial equity, anti-Black racism, and George Floyd. These corporate conversations about race have been coined "uncomfortable" because of the discomfort and annoyance they sometimes cause. There is, understandably, a lack of confidence in our ability to have this conversation. Donnie Bedney interviewed LaDavia Drane, who is now the Chief DEI Officer of Amazon Web Services, on his podcast, *Only Dream Big*. LaDavia talked about bringing the conversation to the workplace and the crucible moments that brought her to this point in her career.[53]

LaDavia explains:

Crucible moment is a term that we use at Amazon—we have a lot of these quirky terms that we use, and this is one. Basically, it is a point at which something in your career turns and you become a transformational leader. You go to that next level.

Even though I had a number of crucible moments in my career, I'll talk to you about one that was most recent for me, because it was a turning point for me before I came into this role (Chief DEI Officer for Amazon Web Services).

Amaud Aubrey had been murdered months previously but it all bubbled up in May (2020), and so I'm at Amazon Web Services, newly transferred over…, and I could tell employees needed to have a conversation about what was happening… We look back now and realize exactly what moment we were in, but back then we didn't know. But in particular, Black men were hurting, this is me seeing black men in my life personally and professionally literally crying, so I knew that we needed to have a conversation.

It's not something that Amazon had done before… so I wrote an email and teed it up. And the response I received was like no other. It wasn't positive.

---

[53] Apple Podcasts. "The Only Dream Big Pod Episode 25 - LaDavia Drane, Amazon Web Services." *Apple Podcasts*, March 10, 2022.
https://podcasts.apple.com/us/podcast/the-only-dream-big-pod-episode-25-ladavia-drane/id1584832853?i=1000553624807.

For the people that I needed to get approval from, or at least I thought I needed approval from— that's another thing I learned, there is something about letting someone inform your decision, consult on your decision, but not necessarily approve your decision—I was seeking approval and it was as if I was asking for something that was just unheard of.

What would be the result? What would be the external response? Is it something that our customers would expect us to do? All these different hypotheticals. So, I remember letting all these different folks weight in, and they would add people, and add more people, add my leader, so I waited for at least 5 hours and when we got to about 10pm, I decided to reply and I gave it everything that I had, and I ended (the email) with "If this is the type of company this is, then I don't belong here and no one of color should feel safe here." And that completely changed the conversation and for me it took courage...

At the moment, I knew I had to take that stance. So for me, that we a crucible moment. We had the conversation... Employees were really excited and they were happy we were willing to have the conversation, then we went on to have two or three other conversations. But in that moment I knew our employees needed us, and I knew exactly what it is they needed, and we needed to deliver for them.

There is Power in Naming the Problem

These conversations may have been exhausting to some, but they did come with a few immediate benefits. They allowed people to be braver. The so-called crazy, sensitive or militant people no longer felt alone. The people who usually get blackballed for calling out racism were finally being heard and respected. These uncomfortable conversations allowed people the opportunity to name the problem, which is racism. When you have the freedom to name the actual problem, people no longer have to dance around it when speaking publicly.

Saying the word "racism" or "white supremacist" in a room full of white executives was considered a landmine in corporate America. You would have to be talking about something that happened decades ago in another state or a different company. Diversity & Inclusion practitioners have been dancing around "racism". They would use biases, unconscious bias, diversity, differences, belonging, sensitivity, and a small percentage were brave enough to say discrimination. The word "racism" seemed to be removed entirely from corporate presentations. There have been a couple of decades of avoiding the term, and most have never even heard of structural or systemic racism.

Correctly naming the issue has power. The power of naming is referred to often when it comes to emotions. Emotional intelligence experts talk about the power of naming your emotions. Denying or avoiding feelings doesn't make them disappear, and it doesn't lessen their impact on us. Naming the emotion gives us the power to choose to take action. This is also true for having open, honest conversations about the problems that exist within corporate America. If you are afraid to name the problem and you choose to deny or avoid it, then you lose the opportunity to take meaningful action from the start. Saying the workplace culture isn't welcoming to diversity, when the issue is actually directly related to racism against Black people, you failed before the initiative even began.

Lay the Educational Foundation for Meaningful Change.

These workplace "conversations" may not create systemic change, but they can help lay the educational foundation for meaningful change. The murder of George Floyd ignited the conversation about racism in America again. Consider these recent polls:

- CBS News June 2020 Poll: 8 in 10 Americans feel discrimination against African-Americans exist today, including half who say there is a lot of discrimination.[54]

- WSJ/NBC June 2020 Poll: Nearly three-quarters of Americans, 71%, believe that race relations are either very or fairly bad, a 16-point increase since February 2020.[55]

---

[54] CBS News. "Americans' Views Shift on Racial Discrimination - CBS News Poll." *CBS News*, June 4, 2020. https://www.cbsnews.com/news/racial-discrimination-americans-views-shift-cbs-news-poll/?ftag=CNM-00-10aab7e.

[55] Siddiqui, Sabrina. "Poll Shows Most Voters Agree Black, Hispanic Americans Face Discrimination." WSJ, July 21, 2020. https://www.wsj.com/articles/majority-of-voters-say-u-s-society-is-racist-as-support-grows-for-black-lives-matter-11595304062.

💡 WSJ/NBC 2020 Poll: Nearly 60% in the survey said that Black people face discrimination, and just over half said so of Hispanics, about double the shares from 2008.[56]

Polls show that most people in America agree that systemic racism and discrimination against Black people exist, and the public's awareness continues to increase. 2020 was a moment of re-education and re-awakening.

It's impossible to eradicate racism in the workplace if we are discouraged to even talk about it. When the corporate culture welcomes these conversations beyond the once-in-a-decade moments of awakening, we could lay the foundation to create change. I hope that these workplace conversations weren't intended as a method to allow people to just blow off steam while the world was in crisis or just a good conversation to make people feel good for the moment. Although therapy sessions are helpful after a crisis, that is not the reason employees were expressing their feeling at these corporate town halls. The aim was for understanding and a call to action. Talking about race is only the start.

We should be proud of the improvements in corporations' statements, pledges, and attitudes because it has given many employees the courage to speak up for social justice at work and through business social media platforms like LinkedIn. But this isn't

---

[56] Siddiqui, Sabrina. "Poll Shows Most Voters Agree Black, Hispanic Americans Face Discrimination." WSJ, July 21, 2020. https://www.wsj.com/articles/majority-of-voters-say-u-s-society-is-racist-as-support-grows-for-black-lives-matter-11595304062.

enough. If we don't do the work to change the system, hope will fade, and all of the 2020-2021 "conversations" will be in vain. These current corporate actions will not be sustainable over the next few years without putting sustainable changes in action.

Questions for Reflection

1. What was your experience listening and participating in the workplace conversation about race?

2. What were the pros and cons of having these conversations at work?

3. Do you and your colleagues feel safe having these conversations at work? Why?

4. Do you want your company to do this again? Why?

5. What would you change about the previous Town Hall?

6. How was the follow up? Were any of the internal concerns addressed?

Chapter 5

Cultural Heritage Month Events & Celebrations

"Two things only the people anxiously desire...bread and circuses"

— **Roman writer**

More organizations are hosting large cultural celebration events for their employees on the days and months of significance, which includes Black History Month, Juneteenth, Pride Month, Indigenous Month, Hispanic Heritage Month, Women's History Month, and many more. These corporate events are intended to recognize customs and traditions of diverse groups and create an environment of inclusion and belonging. They sometimes consist of food, film, music, dance, executive panel discussions, and guest speakers. Much like DEI training events, planning and organizing these celebrations has become a major part of the DEI role at companies.

Juneteenth is one of the many cultural events taking place for employees at work. This new federal holiday commemorates the day on June 19, 1865 when slaves in Galveston, Texas, were finally informed of the end of slavery and the Civil War. CNN shared a list of ways corporate America celebrated this day of significance in 2021. They reported that Apple honored this day of freedom through week-long events for employees designed to educate, build community, and celebrate. Citi Foundation took the event to social media by having Thurgood Marshall College Fund students take over their Instagram account to celebrate Juneteenth. While Google hosted a 2-hour event, spotlighting Black music, history, and storytelling, which included Grammy Award winning singer Erykah Badu.[57]

The growth in cultural events has been partly driven by the increase in the diversity of the U.S. workforce. In the 2019 Inc. article, "3 Ways to Celebrate Your Employees' Cultural Diversity" Maria Haggerty shared how much more diverse the workplace has become and the importance of recognizing and celebrating diversity, "From 1980 to 2020, the percentage of workers in minority groups is projected to double (from 18 percent to 37 percent); the number of Hispanic/Latino workers alone is projected to almost triple (from 6 percent to 17 percent). This is to say that failing to recognize, embrace, and celebrate the diversity of your workforce creates a barrier between you, your employees, and the talent you need to attract."[58] Many executives and DEI consultants believe these events

---

[57] Alcorn, Chauncey. "Companies Are Celebrating Juneteenth in Unique Ways This Week." CNN, June 20, 2021.
https://edition.cnn.com/2021/06/17/business/juneteenth-2021-company-celebrations/index.html.

[58] Haggerty, Maria. "3 Ways to Celebrate Your Employees' Cultural Diversity." Inc.com. December 11, 2019. https://www.inc.com/maria-haggerty/3-ways-to-celebrate-your-employeess-cultural-diversity.html.

bring companies value and positively impacts employee attraction and retention. When asked about cultural events, Daisy Auger-Dominguez, the Chief People Officer at VICE Media, said in the article by author Kathleen Harris, "Helping someone feel seen, heard, and valued is the best way to celebrate them. That's what will lead to greater retention."[59]

Cultural events are a lot of fun. I always enjoyed having a break from the daily grind and taking time to socialize and learn more about the culture of my colleagues during these events. But the question remains: Do company-sponsored culture celebrations at work effectively combat systemic racism and anti-Black racism?

The Myth of Cultural Celebrations' Role in Combating Systemic Racism

Cultural celebrations at work might spark conversations and improve some interpersonal relationships but their impact on combating systemic racism is a big myth. They may even increase awareness, empathy and understand, but historically, the racial inequities continue. We should challenge this common misconception that creating workplace cultural events is an effective strategy to address anti-Black racism.

---

[59] **Harris, Kathleen. "How to Authentically Celebrate Heritage and History Months in the Workplace." 1800Flowers Petal Talk, July 11, 2022.**
https://www.1800flowers.com/blog/business/how-to-celebrate-diversity-at-work.

Loving Black Culture

For example, people of all races, all around the world, have loved and admired African-American culture since the Harlem Renaissance in the 1920s. During this movement of African-American cultural expression, there was a celebration of Black poetry, literature, art, music, and dance in a huge way in America and overseas. Throughout the 20th Century, mainstream America has enjoyed the likes of Langston Hughes, Josephine Baker, Maya Angelou, and Sidney Poitier. This admiration of Black culture continued to peak in the '90s. There were posters of Michael Jordan, Wu-Tang, and 2Pac in non-Black households worldwide and in white college dorm rooms. This "love" of Black entertainment culture continues today. Beyoncé sells out Madison Square Garden in less than a minute, and the majority of the audience is not African-American. But this enjoyment of the Black culture had little if any impact on systemic change in society. In corporate America it has to be actual changes to the workplace experience, not a one-off celebration. After the Juneteenth party, everyone has to return back to their current work environment with the same policies and practices that still haven't been changed.

Symbolic Gesture

Embracing Black culture through a company event or holiday celebration is a good first step towards creating an inclusive environment, but it is just a nice symbolic gesture. In 2020, Danielle Marshall, CEO of Culture Principles, warned businesses in her article, "Symbolic Gestures or Meaningful Change", "I ask for systemic racism to be addressed, you give me a logo change. I again ask for systemic racism to be addressed and you elevate statues, songs, and the removal of confederate flags. I get it, symbols have power, but I caution against getting distracted by the low hanging fruit. These fruit bear wins, though they are not the type of wins that seed future growth. To flourish we need to dig deeper. Systemic racism more broadly impacts policing, education, housing policies, wage gaps, health care, and so on. All of which need to be addressed with solutions of their own."[60]

Mostly Bread and Circuses

When I see all of the inequities and injustices inside and outside of the workplace, I'm not compelled to believe the corporate videos and special celebration events are solving the problem more than they are good marketing. Cultural celebrations can feel like an intentional distraction and window dressing. It can feel like superficial appeasement— a shallow gesture to make you feel better while enduring the hardships of an exclusive culture. It reminds me of the Roman Empire's control strategy of "bread and circuses". Bread and circuses was a phrase used by a Roman writer about the Roman Empire: "Two things only the people anxiously desire: bread and circuses." The Roman Empire kept their citizens happy by distributing cheap free grains and staging huge spectacles. Keep them entertained and fed, and you can reduce the chances of civil unrest. Is your organization feeding its employees grains and spectacles?

---

[60] Culture Principles. "Symbolic Gestures or Meaningful Change –," July 7, 2020. https://www.culture-principles.com/symbolic-gestures-or-meaningful-change/.

If having celebrations is your key tactic to eradicate racism at your company, you are wasting your time, money, energy and offending the very group you are trying to build a positive relationship with. Let's prioritize funding the systemic changes over the celebrations.

Black Space

Black culture events and celebrations may not be an effective strategy to eradicate racism, but it's not always wrong for companies to have them. There are circumstances where having events for Black History Month, Juneteenth, Kwanza, or programs during the year could positively impact the office. If you are leading a company known for extravagant events throughout the year, and your workplace culture is centered on parties and celebrations, it would make sense to do the same for Black culture events. You certainly wouldn't want your Black colleagues to feel excluded.

Another positive aspect of cultural celebrations and social events is that they provide a "Black space" for Black colleagues to meet and connect. These networking events could act as a symbol of a welcoming culture. For example, I recall my first week at a company attending a Black History Month Summit. It felt like I had joined an organization that respects, acknowledges, and welcomes its Black employees. Seeing the support of the CEO in attendance and having the opportunity to network with other Black colleagues had a positive impact on my onboarding experience. These events could be great inspirational experiences for colleagues, but companies must begin making the internal and external events a party with a purpose. As you gather colleagues or the community for these events, use this moment to provide updates on anti-racism policies and practices in action. Don't use events to market your vocal support for change; use them to share the successful action taken.

Cultural Celebrations Are Not Anti-Racism in Action

Celebrations have their benefits, but do not mistake them for corporate anti-racism in action. They are just fun, entertaining, social events. At best, they are cultural awareness campaigns. If your company's answer to the George Floyd protests and your employees' concerns about advancement and Black representation was to have a Juneteenth Celebration for your Black colleagues, you were not listening at all and totally missed the mark.

If your company has an event, here are a few items to keep in mind:

- First, let your volunteer Employee Resource Groups decide whether they plan or participate in a workplace cultural celebration event as a team. Joining a planning committee to create a cultural event should not be mandatory.

- Secondly, if they choose to do an activity, provide them with a budget to do something they find meaningful.

- Lastly, as a company, this is your opportunity to share some data and updates on your specific goals to remove the systemic barrier of racism for your employees, customers, and society. Events could be a great platform to spread the word about your actual anti-racism work in action.

Questions for Reflection

1. List the different cultural celebration events you attended.

2. How was your experience? What did you and your colleagues gain from this experience?

3. Who should be leading, organizing and funding these events?

4. Do you have other ways to provide "Black Spaces", opportunities for colleagues to get inspired, and learn about diverse experiences?

Chapter 6

Black Community Engagement - History and Current State

"We learn from history that we don't learn from history"

— **Desmond Tutu**

History

How much do you know about the history of your organization, industry, or country when it comes anti-Black racism? How many mistakes, out-of-tune actions, and misinformed gestures do you think your organization could avoid if they gained knowledge of the past instead of trying to ignore history? What is your organization's historical relationship with the Black community? Was it a positive relationship?

It doesn't matter if your organization is global, national, regional, or even local, you have a relationship with the Black community. Regardless of your organization's size, location, or years in business, it's likely the Black community has experienced your company, and it is vital to the health and future of your business to have a good understanding of that relationship— past and present.

Your Sector: Healthcare

The history of your sector or industry also matters. For example, the healthcare industry struggled to convince Black people to take the COVID19 vaccine in 2021. It's important to know why there is so much distrust of the healthcare industry and the U.S. government. The people involved in the COVID19 Vaccine rollout were not part of the infamous 1932-1972 Tuskegee Syphilis Experiment of course, but this experiment still impacts the relationship with the Black community 50 years later. This terrible history still is one of the leading reasons for the mistrust. In February 2021, during the early rollout of the COVID-19 vaccination, most white people were getting the shot while Black people hesitated to participate. A February 2021 article from NPR.com explained, "It has played out in early data that show a stark disparity in whom is getting shots in this country— more than 60% going to white people, and less than 6% to African Americans. The mistrust is rooted in history, including the infamous U.S. study of syphilis that left Black men in Tuskegee, Ala., to suffer from the disease." [61]

Unfortunately, the Tuskegee Syphilis Experiment wasn't the only healthcare violence against the Black community, but it is one of the most known incidences and it had a significant impact. Wouldn't you want to know if there were incidents in your industry or company's history that caused mistrust? You can't confront anti-

---

[61] Elliott, Debbie. "In Tuskegee, Painful History Shadows Efforts To Vaccinate African Americans." NPR.org, February 16, 2021.
https://www.npr.org/2021/02/16/967011614/in-tuskegee-painful-history-shadows-efforts-to-vaccinate-african-americans.

Black racism in your workplace and community without knowing your history. We should know if our organization participated in acts of Black exploitation, as well as the times when our organization stood up against racism.

Your Sector: Prison Industrial Complex

Some companies have made a fortune by exploiting African-American prisoners and their families. In the early 20th century, many companies gained incredible wealth through convict leasing. According to Douglas Blackmon, in his book *Slavery by Another Name*, "The growth of U.S. Steel and its subsidiaries in the South was partly dependent on the labor of cheaply paid black workers and exploited convicts… U.S. Steel had agreements with more than 20 counties in Alabama to obtain the labor of its prisoners, often paying locals nine dollars a month for workers who would be forced into their mines through a system of convict leasing."[62]

U.S. Steel, along with many other companies, exploited Black prisoners who were primarily victims of the South's racist Black Codes and imprisoned by vagrancy laws. Blackmon shared in an interview that U.S. Steel acknowledges they participated in convict leasing but since it was 100 years ago, they believe it is irrelevant now.[63] Companies that are truly genuine about wanting to champion

---

[62] Wikipedia contributors. "U.S. Steel." Wikipedia, November 3, 2022. https://en.wikipedia.org/wiki/U.S._Steel.
[63] Newsweek Staff. "Book: American Slavery Continued Until 1941." Newsweek, July 1, 2010. https://www.newsweek.com/book-american-slavery-continued-until-1941-93231.

diversity and inclusion and eradicate racism, should start with righting their own wrongs, not dismissing them.

U.S. Steel published their first Diversity & Inclusion report on August 2022. They highlighted the progress made in their D&I efforts and awards. Ironically, they were also recognized by Ethisphere as one of the 2022 World's Most Ethical Companies, while never acknowledging the damage they had done to the Black community.[64]

Your Sector: Financial Institutions

Corporate America's past transgressions doesn't stop at exploiting prison labor. The banking industry has also discriminated against Black communities through redlining. For decades the federal government and U.S. Banks would deny mortgages to Black families. Ta-Nehisi Coates highlights this in his famous article, *The Case for Reparations*, "Neighborhoods where black people lived were rated "D" and were usually ineligible for F.H.A. backing. They were colored in red... Redlining went beyond FHA-backed loans and spread to the entire mortgage industry, which was already rife with racism, excluding black people from most legitimate means of obtaining a mortgage." [65]

In 1977 President Jimmy Carter signed into law the Community Reinvestment Act. This act was passed to stop redlining, which is discriminatory credit practices against Black people and other

---

[64] Business Wire. "U. S. Steel Publishes 2022 Diversity, Equity and Inclusion Report," August 9, 2022. https://www.businesswire.com/news/home/20220808005766/en/
[65] Coates, Ta-Nehisi. "The Case for Reparations by Ta-Nehisi Coates." The Atlantic, February 10, 2022. https://www.theatlantic.com/magazine/archive/2014/06/the-case-for-reparations/361631/.

disenfranchised groups. This sad history is a major part of the financial industry's relationship with the Black community. The Community Reinvestment Act requires federal regulators to assess how well each bank fulfills its obligations of lending and investing in Low to Moderate income communities. [66]

This abusive banking relationship continued in 2008 but in the form of reverse-redlining. Reverse-redlining is the illegal practice of extending credit on unfair terms in a particular community, also known as predatory lending. According to Richard Rothstein, author of *The Color of Law*, it was African-American communities that mortgage brokers targeted for subprime lending during the pre-2008 housing bubble [67]. In 2008, Cleveland sued a large group of subprime lenders, including Citicorp, Bank of America, Wells Fargo, and others. [68]

Regardless of the name of the bank, this is part of the Black experience with banks, and this is just a slice of the negative experiences. As banks strategize on strengthening their relationship with the Black community, they can't ignore or dismiss past actions. With any improvement program, the first step is to take an honest look at the current state, and the past experience impacts the

---

[66] Coates, Ta-Nehisi. "The Case for Reparations by Ta-Nehisi Coates." The Atlantic, February 10, 2022. https://www.theatlantic.com/magazine/archive/2014/06/the-case-for-reparations/361631/.
[67] Rothstein, Richard, Color of Law: A Forgotten History of How Our Government Segregated America. (New York, NY 2017)
[68] Pierog, Karen. "Cleveland Sues 21 Banks Over Mortgage Foreclosures." U.S., January 12, 2008. https://www.reuters.com/article/sppage012-n11294432-oisbn/cleveland-sues-21-banks-over-mortgage-foreclosures-idUSN1129443220080111.

community's opinions and behavior today. History matters, and it is essential to your organization's development, growth, and success.

United States History

Robert Foster, retired Northrop Gruman senior leader and Business Resource Group lead, and Master Coach with the Skinner Institute, shared his thoughts with me on the impact of history and America's relationship with the Black community.

> *Foster shared, "When you talk about systemic racism, you are talking about society. You are talking about structural. When you look at Plessy vs Ferguson in 1896, the supreme court said separate but equal is constitutional. Remember this is the legal system that decided this. Then you have until 1954, all of this time when separate but equal is considered legal. Then you have a second-class citizen baked into society. In 1954, you have Brown vs. Board of Education, where they say no that is unconstitutional. But the same institution, the Supreme Court, they are one that decided that. Then you get to 1964, Congress puts in the Civil Rights Act of 1964. "Diversity" didn't really start coming into the conversation until the early 1970s. People say racism is a social construct and it's true. It's because this person in power says it's so. Who's still in power? It is going to take time for white privilege to play out."*

Racism and white privilege have been deeply embedded in American society for so long. The legal structure, led by the people in power, intentionally created bias, discrimination and anti-Black racism. This may be a grim reality but the silverlining is if people in power could create system of racism, those in leadership now have the ability to create a new system of anti-racism.

The Current State: Data and the Corporate Approach to Driving Change

Current State of Racial Equity

When I worked for The Gallup Organization, a global analytics and advice firm, we conducted employee engagement surveys to assess the culture of organizations. For the key survey question items, we would begin slicing and dicing the data to identify where the elements of employee engagement and disengagement existed within the organization. We left no stone unturned. As a human capital consultant, I would compare the data year over year by department, gender, race, tenure, level of formal education, and any data metric available. We would even dig deep into the intersections of the metrics. For example, women age 25-35 with 1-5 years tenure in the marketing department responded this way compared to other survey responses.

Even though we knew we shouldn't try to take on the impossible task of analyzing every possible data cut, also known as "boiling the ocean", we sometimes would still try. We were always searching for that gem—that needle in the haystack. However, the "best practice" of analyzing data is to start with a hypothesis and ask the right questions first. What problems are you trying to solve?

The point is, if you know what you are looking for, you don't have to "boil the ocean". If you're only looking at high-level diversity metrics like P.O.C. (people of color), you are not trying to understand the Black experience at your organization; you are ignoring it. Only sharing broad diversity & inclusion numbers does not tell the whole story or any clear story for that matter. Organizations have been receiving rewards and recognition for their work in D&I but continue to struggle with addressing the systematic racism impacting their Black employees. Which begs the question, why have so many organizations decided not to report diversity metrics by race?

Be Transparent with the Black Diversity Data

Companies have to do a deeper dive into the data, if they are serious about improving race-related matters in the workplace. For example, what does it mean when a company says their staff is 80% diverse? It only means that 20% are white, male, Christian, cisgender, heterosexual, without a disability. And companies that claim to be 50% racially diverse only means that 50% of their employees are white. It doesn't always mean their racial diversity includes the black or brown community.

Coca-Cola has had a long history of dealing with racial discrimination since its historic $192.5 million class-action lawsuit. After the company made progress, increasing their Black executive representation from 1.5% in 1998 to 15% in 2000, the number fell back down to 8% in 2020. According to the Wall Street Journal article, "Coke's diversity push-started as an effort to address discrimination against Black employees and broadened over the years to encompass gender and other races and groups."[69]

I commend Coke for its efforts to make the organization more equitable for all. Fairness for all does not have to take away from the progress of Black people. Inclusion is infinite. My father kept this quote on his living room wall: "Love is the only thing that can be divided without being diminished." That also goes for inclusion and equity. With that said, Coke has work to do to improve the numbers, but unlike many other companies, they are at least tracking the numbers. The goal must be to continue tracking and monitoring all of the key demographics that concern your organization. Organizations must be transparent with their D&I data related to Black colleagues and not hide it behind the overall diversity number.

The End of the "Business Results" Approach to Supporting Racial Equity

Over the last 20 years, DEI practitioners have shifted their approach to finding support for their industry by focusing on the power of diversity of thought and moving away from the social justice agenda. They have shared with leaders that diversity of thought will result in innovation, creativity, and a positive financial impact. They told executives it's not only the right thing to do, but it's good for business. They also leveraged the 2015 Mckinsey's Diversity Matters report.[70]

---

[69] Maloney, Jennifer and Weber, Lauren. "Coke's Elusive Goal: Boosting Its Black Employees." WSJ, December 16, 2020. https://www.wsj.com/articles/coke-resets-goal-of-boosting-black-employees-after-20-year-effort-loses-ground-11608139999.
[70] Hunt, Dame Vivian, Dennis Layton, and Sara Prince. "Why Diversity Matters." McKinsey & Company, March 12, 2021.

This report became popular in the DEI world because it found that companies in the top quartile for racial and ethnic diversity are 35 percent more likely to have financial returns above their respective national industry medians.

What is the data really saying? First, this shows a correlation, not a causation. Considering all the factors that drive financial outcomes throughout the year, the diversity of the leadership is one of many, not the sole reason. And the direction of the correlation was not determined. Could it be that companies with high financial outcomes are more inclusive and more willing to bring in racially diverse leaders? Next, you have to be cautious when comparing top quartiles vs. bottom quartiles or averages or medians. These studies do mask the variances in the data. At the individual level, you will likely find some organizations in the top quartile for racial diversity that did not outperform the national industry medians.

The real takeaway should be that diverse boards *can* outperform the average organization; not that they *will* outperform them. D&I practitioners are misusing this study when they suggest diverse boards guarantee success. Instead, leaders should use this as the foundation to convince executives that being racially diverse doesn't have to impact the bottom line negatively. They don't have to choose whether to outperform their competitors or create an inclusive culture; they could have it both ways, and this is why I still do consider this a seminal study in the advancement of D&I. At the end of the day,

---

https://www.mckinsey.com/capabilities/people-and-organizational-performance/our-insights/why-diversity-matters.

regardless of the way the story is told, it still hasn't been enough to push organizations to address systemic racism. However, this Mckinsey study has provided CEOs with a sense of comfort when saying they believe in diversity, but it hasn't been compelling enough to drive most CEOs to take meaningful actions.

Three Reasons Why the Social Justice Approach Is Replacing the Diversity of Thought Approach

While this Diversity of Thought movement provided a few benefits to D&I, there have been many adverse impacts. First, this movement takes us away from our end goal—to end discrimination and racial inequity. Shouldn't fairness and justice be enough? If increasing Black representation at your company doesn't result in greater financial gains, is that a reason to stop removing the barriers blocking the hiring and promotion of Black people? The Diversity of Thought rhetoric sounds pretty close to saying, "I know your organization doesn't value fairness and respect for all people, but let me show you how it could make your company money."

So far, the Diversity of Thought movement hasn't grabbed the attention of CEOs when it comes to Black progress; but the protest and civil unrest have. The 2020 protests forced many companies to look in the mirror and set goals related to Black representation. They began allocating money and resources to make improvements inside the organization and through philanthropy. We haven't seen this type of goal setting and focus since the early 80s. In the 80s and 90s, we didn't dance around the primary issue —racism and discrimination— as we do today. We didn't hide behind creativity, innovation, diverse thought, and financial outcomes. We should go back to being honest about the issue and what we are demanding. Is it social justice or our deep passion for diverse ideas?

When we lead with "diversity of thought," there are so many ways a company could improve their diversity of thought without even giving a thought to the Black community. Even during the 2020 protest, I didn't see one sign saying, "We need Diversity of Thought." No, the protests were not a fight for diverse ideas. They were fighting for the eradication of racism.

Secondly, it pushes a diversity for everyone approach, which further dilutes and alters the original goals and meaning of D&I. Apple's V.P. of Diversity, Denise Young, learned the hard way about this. In 2017, at the One Young World Summit, Young Smith said, "There can be 12 white, blue-eyed, blond men in a room and they're going to be diverse too because they're going to bring different life experience and life perspective to the conversation" and she went on to say, "Diversity is the human experience…I get a little bit frustrated when diversity or the term diversity is tagged to the people of color, or women, or the LGBT."[71]

Smith later apologized for her comments and stepped down six months later. "Diversity of Thought" and "All Diversity Matters" approaches go beyond executives being scared or weak. Of course,

---

[71] Weller, Chris. "Apple's VP of Diversity Says '12 White, Blue-Eyed, Blonde Men in a Room' Can Be a Diverse Group." Business Insider, October 11, 2017.
https://www.businessinsider.in/apples-vp-of-diversity-says-12-white-blue-eyed-blonde-men-in-a-room-can-be-a-diverse-group/articleshow/61044332.cms.

the hypothetical group of 12 white men could have 12 unique experiences. They could differ by education, geographic location, rural vs. city, different European ethnicity, age, professional expertise, married vs. single, diverse ability, etc. However, are these types of differences the primary goal of your DE&I program? Is this the problem they are trying to solve at Apple or other organizations? This is why the Diversity of Thought movement should be abandoned. It has allowed leaders to completely ignore racial diversity, which is counterproductive when you aim to eradicate anti-Black racism from your workplace.

Questions for Reflection

1. What other industries, and company have a dark history with the Black/African American community?

2. Which industries or companies are doing a good job restoring justice and righting some of their wrongs from the past?

3. What should your company be doing to repair or build a better relationship with the Black/African-American community? What have they done so far?

4. How does your organization measure racial equity for the Black employee, customers, and the community?

5. How do you feel about the Diversity of Thought approach? Pros and cons?

Chapter 7

Shaping the World for the Better

Part 1 - Institutional and Economic Power

"If you are trying to shape the world for the better, you are engaging in a political act – which raises the question of whether you are employing an appropriately political process to guide the shaping"

— **Anand Giridharadas**

Society is asking corporations to act in the same manner we expect good American citizens to behave, which is to treat others— their stakeholders— with respect and dignity. These stakeholders include shareholders, employees, customers, suppliers, community, government, and the media. But today, only being concerned with your behavior and business strategy isn't good enough to be a great corporate citizen. Now, society also expects organizations to take the additional steps of speaking up and taking action when they see others commit acts of injustice.

Major League Baseball's Political Action against the State of Georgia

Major League Baseball engaged in a political act when they moved their All-Star game out of Georgia in March 2021 after the Georgia state government passed a significant voting law restricting voting access, which would considerably impact the Black vote. The new voting restrictions included stricter voter identification requirements for absentee balloting, limits drop boxes in the Atlanta metro area, expanded legislative control over the elections, and criminalizing the act of providing food and water to anyone waiting in line. [72] Making the act of giving food and water a crime is a clear indicator of whose vote the government is attempting to restrict. While many African-American Georgians waited in 5-to-10-hour voting lines for the 2020 Presidential election, groups provided food, drink, music, and entertainment to help Black voters stay in these long lines. The government witnessed a specific action done by Black people, and then decided to make it a crime. Criminalizing Black culture is an old and often-used tactic of oppression in America.

When this new voting rights law passed, Delta, Coca-Cola, and other Atlanta-based companies condemned the law immediately. Even the Levi Strauss (based in California) CEO Chip Bergh called this law "racist," and opposing politicians said it should be called Jim

---

[72] Montanaro, Domenico. "MLB's Move Out Of Georgia Is The Latest In A Line Of Political Boycotts." NPR.org, April 12, 2021.
https://www.npr.org/2021/04/12/985974670/mlbs-move-out-of-georgia-is-the-latest-in-a-line-of-political-boycotts.

Crow 2.0.[73] But this escalated beyond the corporate statements against this bill when things shifted from words to actions. On April 2, 2021, the Major League Baseball Commissioner, Robert Manfred, announced Atlanta would no longer host the 2021 MLB All-Star Game due to the league's stance against Georgia's new voting law restrictions.[74] Essentially, they sent the message that they would not participate in helping Georgia gain economic growth if they continued to pass anti-Black policies.

According to Cobb County Travel and Tourism, the move of the All-Star Game from Atlanta to Denver cost the county $100 million in tourism dollars.[75] Unfortunately, the actions of the MLB and other companies did not move the Georgia politicians to change the law during the summer of 2021, but their voices and actions were seen and felt financially.

What is your institutional power and how are you using it? Institutional power is defined as the power used by corporations to control other groups and direct their behavior through rewards and punishments like the allocation of resources.[76] The MLB saw Georgia

---

[73] Twitter. "Poppy Harlow On," April 9, 2021. https://twitter.com/PoppyHarlowCNN/status/1380530742577487875.
[74] Reimann, Nicholas. "Judge Denies Request To Force MLB All-Star Game Back To Atlanta." Forbes, June 11, 2021. https://www.forbes.com/sites/nicholasreimann/2021/06/10/judge-denies-request-to-force-mlb-all-star-game-back-to-atlanta/?sh=4beb65785d8e.
[75] Chen, Natasha, Melissa Alonso, and Alaa Elassar. "MLB's Decision to Move Its All-Star Game out of Georgia Will Have a $100 Million Impact on the State, Tourism Official Says." CNN, April 3, 2021. https://edition.cnn.com/2021/04/03/us/mlb-all-star-game-relocation-lost-money-economic-impact/index.html.
[76] "Study.Com | Take Online Courses. Earn College Credit. Research Schools, Degrees & Careers," n.d. https://study.com/academy/lesson/institutional-power-definition-lesson-quiz.html.

commit an act of injustice, and they exercised their institutional power in an attempt to bring justice. Does your organization know the power it holds? Are they willing to use it?

Economic Power and Divestment: The long game

There is a point when large institutions - churches, universities, nonprofits, government, and corporations - have to leverage their economic power to drive change despite the immediate risks. One of the best examples of economic power in action is the divestment in South Africa to help end Apartheid. The September 18, 1986, L.A. Times article reads:

"Coca-Cola, the dominant soft drink marketer in South Africa and a major symbol of U.S. corporate involvement there, thus will join a growing list of U.S. firms pulling out of the nation amid mounting furor over its apartheid system of racial discrimination." The article continued with this statement from the then Coca-Cola COO, Donald R. Keough: "Our decision to complete the process of disinvestment is a statement of our opposition to apartheid and of our support for the economic aspirations of black South Africans."[77]

Coca-Cola's statement and divestment from South Africa became known as one of the major nails in the coffin of Apartheid. Later that same year came U.S. congressional sanctions against South Africa. As a result, in the early 1990s, all of the components of

---

[77] Sing, Bill. "Coca-Cola Acts to Cut All Ties With S. Africa." Los Angeles Times, March 12, 2019. https://www.latimes.com/archives/la-xpm-1986-09-18-mn-11241-story.html.

Apartheid came to an end. But the fight in the U.S. to end Apartheid didn't begin with Coca-Cola.

It started in the '60s with protests and demonstrations on college campuses.[78] Then in the '70s, the Universities divested stocks of companies doing business in South Africa. Next, in 1977 Reverend Leon Sullivan, a board member of General Motors, created a list of provisions for corporations called the Sullivan principles. This was designed with the hopes for corporations to pledge to enforce equal treatment of Black employees. The pledges helped start a movement but it wasn't enough to push South Africa to change. Similar to today's corporate pledges (ex: CEO Action for Diversity & Inclusion[79]).

Then the stakes were raised. In 1982, Millions of Black workers boycotted South African jobs, and the call to boycott Coca-Cola and other companies doing business in South Africa picked up around the world. Companies felt the economic pressure of the world and were forced to change and divest from South Africa. As a result, there was a deterioration of business conditions in South Africa, and they had

---

[78] Times, The New York. "Million Black Workers Boycott South Africa Jobs." The New York Times, June 7, 1988. https://www.nytimes.com/1988/06/07/world/million-black-workers-boycott-south-africa-jobs.html.
[79] CEO Action for Diversity & Inclusion. "Purpose," n.d. https://www.ceoaction.com/purpose/.

to either end Apartheid or be isolated by the world and watch their economy crumble[80,81].

I know there is much more to the story of Apartheid South Africa beyond this book's scope, but this was a great example of institutional and economic power in action. This corporate stance against racism was a special, historical moment for freedom and corporate social responsibility. But for those corporate leaders looking for instant results without any sacrifice, keep in mind this divestment strategy took over 30 years. This was a lifetime commitment of courage and endurance. Dismantling systemic racism is not a brief summer volunteer activity.

There were naysayers on the plan for corporations to divest from South Africa. Many argued that divesting from the country would hurt the protesters, the very people you are trying to help. Opposer of the boycott cried the corporation would be taking jobs and income out of the country. Some also made the case that U.S. companies could do more by staying in South Africa by influencing the South African government to improve the treatment of Black people, and by doing business there, they could ensure fair employment conditions and receive equal pay through their corporate

---

[80] Investopedia. "Protest Divestment and the End of Apartheid," July 3, 2022. https://www.investopedia.com/articles/economics/08/protest-divestment-south-africa.asp.
[81] Larson, Zeb. "The Sullivan Principles: South Africa, Apartheid, and Globalization." OUP Academic, March 17, 2020. https://academic.oup.com/dh/article-abstract/44/3/479/5809124?redirectedFrom=fulltext.

policies.[82] These are the same arguments we still hear today in the US when we talk about boycotting a state (ex: Florida after the not guilty verdict when Trayvon Martin was murdered) or a company.

The slow strategy of reform - pledges and pleas for change - was a good start, but ultimately it did not prove to be effective enough. The protests, Universities divesting from stocks, and the Sullivan principle pledges didn't push the South African government to end racial discrimination, but when U.S. corporations used economic power to negatively impact their economy, things changed. Trying to connect to the South African government's hearts, minds, and morality didn't work, but punishing their economy did. Five years after U.S. government sanctions and U.S. corporation's divestment South Africa's apartheid system ended.

When the naysayers of the MLB boycott claim that when the MLB moved the All-star game to Denver, they punished the wrong people— small businesses owners, workers, the tourism industry— you have to consider the long-term impact, not just the short-term impact. The argument that you could "do more good" by continuing business relationships with someone committing injustices than you can by boycotting them has not always been valid. Many people will have to sacrifice to send the message to the Georgia government, or other states and the federal government, that these injustices will not be tolerated. Hit them where it hurts, their pockets.

---

[82] **Investopedia. "Protest Divestment and the End of Apartheid," July 3, 2022.** https://www.investopedia.com/articles/economics/08/protest-divestment-south-africa.asp.

Demonstrations and Political Action Come with Risks and Backlash

Before we tackle how your organization could use its power to fight against anti-Black racism in society, let's start with looking at the risks and some examples of power used at the individual level. As the saying goes, freedom isn't free.

Athletes and celebrities have done demonstrations in support of the Black community for decades. Olympic medalists Tommy Smith and John Carlos raised their black-gloved fists in the air at the 1968 Olympics to raise awareness of Black suffering in America. As a result, both of their careers ended. This demonstration even destroyed the career of the white Australian runner, Peter Norman, because he refused to denounce Tommy and John's actions.

Colin Kaepernick took a knee in a demonstration to raise awareness of police violence against the Black community, and it was met with backlash by the National Football League and sports media. In return, he was blackballed from the NFL and never played again after being cut from the San Francisco 49ers.

In 2017 the show *Black-ish* had an episode raising awareness about the Juneteenth holiday and why it is celebrated, and it was met with praise. In this musical episode, they had songs re-educating America on the history of emancipation and slavery. However, when the show's creator, Kenya Barris, tried to push it further with an episode addressing the current race relations in the U.S. - The treatment of Colin Kaepernick and Charlotteville riots – the ABC executives shelved the episode. This resulted in Kenya Barris leaving

From Promises to Progress

the network because of "creative differences".[83] Executives are comfortable talking about the race relations of 100 years ago that they do not have the power to change or impact, but they are reluctant to address the current conditions we do have the ability to influence.

Musicians have also made socially conscious songs. Some artists started with fun dance music then later switched to songs that raised awareness of racism and inequalities. Marvin Gaye surprised his fans when he stepped away from the love songs like "Let's Get It On" and brought the world the album "What's Going On". And Sam Cooke's song "A Change Gonna Come" was released soon after his death. Sam hesitated to release a song supporting Black liberation because he knew anything controversial was a career risk.

These demonstrations were all considered risky career moves that could make the American mainstream society - the white customers, executives and partners - uncomfortable.

Takeaways:

- 💡 They used their celebrity power and art to build awareness and encourage others to join the fight against racism. Their platform and talent had the power to reach and influence the thoughts of millions. They put their values into action through their athleticism, music, and art.

---

[83] Barnes, Brooks. "Kenya Barris, Creator of 'Black-Ish,' Will Leave ABC Studios in August." The New York Times, July 30, 2018.
https://www.nytimes.com/2018/07/27/business/media/kenya-barris-abc-netflix.html.

- If it doesn't feel risky or scary, then you're not demonstrating or protesting. True solidarity and support for the Black community come with risks. In these examples, ABC and the NFL weren't willing to take that risk.

- Individual demonstrations may not create the change you desire, but they could spark the change we need. When individuals, groups, and systems leverage their power for good, the world starts looking different.

Questions for Reflection

1 Could you name other examples where companies got involved in political action like Major League Baseball did with the state of Georgia?

2 List your pros and cons of divesting.

3 What backlash have you faced from the public when implementing racial equity initiatives?

4 What is your organization's institutional power? What resources and influence do you hold?

5 Do you have any new products, services, or employee volunteer programs that were developed in response to addressing anti-Black racism?

Part 2 - Political Power

Today's Corporate Demonstrations and Political Action

Corporate demonstrations work well when companies include the Black experience in the work they are already doing. Nike demonstrated support through their socially and politically charged "Dream Crazy" commercial. This commercial launched during the height of the Colin Kaepernick controversy, where the NFL was still blackballing Colin for the second year because he was taking a knee during the national anthem to protest racial injustice and police brutality. In 2018, companies avoided Colin like the plague, but Colin did the voiceover for this Nike commercial which said, "Believe in something even if it means sacrificing everything." This demonstration resulted in an initial dip in their stock, but the stock bounced back shortly after, and in 2019 Nike received an Emmy for the commercial.[84] The commercial was extremely risky at the time, and Nike was rewarded for its courageous stance.

Google is also known for its demonstrations of recognition and support through its Google Doodles. The doodles recognize historical events, birthdays, Independence Day, etc., and their doodles have not shied away from including Black history and discussing racism beyond the month of February. I appreciate when

---

[84] Mitra, Mallika. "Nike Won Its First 'outstanding Commercial' Emmy in 17 Years for an Ad Featuring Colin Kaepernick." CNBC, September 17, 2019.
https://www.cnbc.com/2019/09/16/nike-wins-emmy-for-ad-featuring-colin-kaepernick.html.

they recognized the lesser-known giants of history, like Carter G Woodson, the founder of Black History Week, and the Association for the Study of African American Life and History. But on July 28, 2017, the Google Doodles got more political when they commemorated the 100th anniversary of the Silent Parade, where nearly 10,000 African American children, women, and men marched in silence in one of the first mass protests against lynching and anti-Black violence in the U.S.[85] The doodles are used to build awareness of specific people and events, and they took the time to recognize this historic American event.

Awareness campaigns like the Nike and Google example are a great start, but for companies that are branding themselves as purpose-driven and socially conscious, there has to be more. Roles in Social Impact, Corporate Citizenship, Corporate Social Responsibility, and Environmental Social Governance continue to grow, and society continues to ask companies to do more in the fight against racial inequity. As your company begins its journey to improve the world through its products, services, philanthropy, and volunteers, it must also consider getting involved with public policies.

Public policy on both the state and federal level have the greatest impact in dismantling systemic racism in America. It has been racist, anti-Black policies at all levels of the government over the last 150 years that created the current structure we live in today. Fortune 500 companies already have government affairs departments and

---

[85] "100th Anniversary of the Silent Parade," n.d. https://www.google.com/doodles/100th-anniversary-of-the-silent-parade.

lobbyists fighting for the company's economic and political interests, so saying "we don't want to get political" is a weak excuse. As Anund Giridharadas said in his influential book, *Winner Take All, the elite charade of changing the world*, "If you are trying to shape the world for the better, you are engaging in a political act." [86]

As an organization dedicated to improving the world and fighting against anti-Black racism, you must use all of your levers of power: institutional, economic, and political power. Identify where your organization is well-positioned to make a meaningful impact, and put it into action. We can't go another 50 years re-implementing the same old diversity & inclusion and social responsibility approaches and hope for different results.

How Should Your Company Demonstrate Public Support for the Black Community and Fight against Racism? What Actions Can You Take to Fight for a Better World?

During the 2020 protests for justice, organizations made statements supporting Black lives and shared their action plans to address anti-Black racism. When Derek Chauvin was found guilty, most corporate leaders expressed relief at the guilty verdict and said the fight for racial justice must continue. But what does "continuing" entail?

---

[86] Giridharasdas, Anand, Winner Take All: The Elite Charade of Changing the World. (New York, NY, 2018)

Now, the George Floyd Justice in Policing Act is on the table. The George Floyd Justice in Policing Act addresses a wide range of policies regarding policing practices and law enforcement accountability. It lowers the criminal intent standard from willful to knowing or reckless, limits qualified immunity as a defense and many other remedies. This bill passed in the House of Representatives but has not been voted on yet in the Senate.[87] There are many questions regarding what to do next. There are some that even consider the George Floyd Justice in Policing Act to be a weak approach to structure change. I won't debate about its strength, but this act sitting in the Senate does address police violence against the Black or Brown community, and we shouldn't miss this opportunity to make some gains in racial equity.

IBM's Corporate Social Responsibility Stance

IBM sent a letter to the U.S. House of Representatives showing support for the George Floyd Justice in Policing Act. The IBM site explains, "Last summer, IBM CEO Arvind Krishna urged leaders in Congress to take concrete steps that can advance racial justice in three areas: policing reform, responsible use of technology, and expanding access to skills and opportunity."[88] As of September 2022, the talks of passing the George Floyd Policing Act in the Senate have stalled. One of the critical issues gridlocking this vital bill that already passed in the House in March 2021 is the proposal to reform Qualified

---

[87] Congress.gov. https://www.congress.gov/bill/116th-congress/house-bill/7120
[88] IBM Policy. "IBM on the George Floyd Justice in Policing Act of 2021," April 15, 2022. https://www.ibm.com/policy/police-reform-bill/.

Immunity. Currently, Qualified Immunity shields police officers from civil liability for misconduct. Republicans aren't willing to make any meaningful reforms to this issue, and Democrats aren't willing to push through a watered down, ineffective policy.[89]

IBM has publicly stated they support a change to immunity laws so that people can seek damages when police officers violate their constitutional rights. IBM has even held itself accountable for their contributions to the over-policing culture through their facial recognition technology and decided to get out of that business when the racial biases in the technology became national news.[90]

What Should Companies Be Doing Now to Shape Society?

I interviewed Eboni Riley to get her take on what companies can do to shape society for the better. As the Washington Bureau Chief for the National Action Network, Eboni organized the Commitment March on Washington on August 28, 2020, with over 250k attendees, including George Floyd's family. This was a call for thousands of people to come to Washington DC to demonstrate advocacy for comprehensive police accountability reform, the Census, and mobilizing voters for the November elections.

---

[89] Greve, Joan. "Sweeping George Floyd Police Reform Bill Stalls as Talks Collapse." The Guardian, September 23, 2021. https://www.theguardian.com/us-news/2021/sep/22/us-police-reform-bill-congress-bipartisan-talks.
[90] Hirsch, Lauren. "IBM Gets out of Facial Recognition Business, Calls on Congress to Advance Policies Tackling Racial Injustice." CNBC, June 9, 2020. https://www.cnbc.com/2020/06/08/ibm-gets-out-of-facial-recognition-business-calls-on-congress-to-advance-policies-tackling-racial-injustice.html.

Eboni Riley is now the Senior Vice President of Policy and Strategic Partnerships. The highest-ranking woman in the history of National Action Network. I first met Eboni in January 2020, as classmates in the Skinner Institute's Master Series for Distinguished Leaders Program. Eboni spoke with me about the march:

I came into this movement in 2011. I was drawn to this movement because I was impacted.

When my boss advocated for Trayvon Martin who was already buried for a month, that was the reason it was elevated to television. So when people have an issue with marching it's because they are not educated on why that's something we do. There are many opinions on whether marching is good or bad, but we need to have some sort of amplification on an issue putting pressure on those that have the authority to change things... Many times, the media drives the narrative on issues, and sometimes grassroots organizations and other folks want to be helpful but are sometimes harmful. They lose sight of why we are upset. We are upset because this Black man (George Floyd) did not get due process of the law. There was excessive force, and there were no real sanctions for those that were involved. And people are tired of seeing this.

I asked Eboni for her thoughts on how companies should get involved in political action and what role they should play. Eboni explained:

I sometimes find it troubling how companies choose to and what issues they choose to get involved with but I do think voting is very important because it covers all issues, voting impacts them all. Education, healthcare, employment, and immigration, so it made a lot of sense when companies stepped up and spoke out about Georgia's voting rights issue...Voting is so powerful. You can't talk about any issue without voting. Because some of these folks that are with specific companies have to abide by legislation, we still want equal protection under the law, we still want to be active and engage with who we put in office, so we want to make sure they are adding those regulations to companies, if necessary, that may have a poor history.

I say, great you want to help, let us take a look at your company. Do you have a plan to protect your employees during voting? You say you care about the election and you want to recruit us, but can your employees have a paid day off to go practice democracy?

Eboni also shared a few corporate myths and missteps we should keep in mind:

1 **Companies think sharing their diversity reports is enough.** *Many companies are proud of their diversity reports that are poor. Companies celebrate going from 1% to 4% minorities in 5 years, and they think that is good. You mean at this day and time you couldn't find enough Black people sufficient enough to fill roles at your company? And what programs do you have in place for upward*

mobility for folks that may have come in on an entry-job level to be trained to be able to fill those positions in the future?

2 **People think companies don't have the budget to address a specific issue.** *They have the budget for what you are asking for; they just don't want to give it to you. They invest in what they want to see change. There are companies that say they only can give you $250k, and I'll see them give $1 million to another company or group for a totally different cause.*

3 **A common misstep is when their giving isn't authentic.** *Here's the other thing that's very controversial. You cannot give effort, money, and time, to a vendor, consultant, or organization that is advocating for a specific community, but the person you are doing the deal with isn't of that community. Authentic voices matter, and a lot of times during get-out-to-vote time, and I'm not trying to say anything bad here but, white progressives jump in front of other minority groups and collect funding because they have an advantage on infrastructure, or people pouring into them then they go off and say they have all these things. And they don't even align or talk to other organizations that are in the community, live in the community, and are of the community daily. It's very important for companies to align their selves with authentic voices and relationships and that's how you become allies.*

Questions for Reflection

1 What legislative bills should corporations rally around? The Crown Act, the George Floyd Justice in Policing Act, or others? Why?

2 How are you deepening your relationship with the Black organizations you funded? How have you taken it from transactional to a real partnership?

3 What are you doing to help your employees exercise their right to vote?

Chapter 8

Repurposing Successful Models and Frameworks to Address Anti-Black Racism

"You may not always have a comfortable life and you will not always be able to solve all of the world's problems at once, but don't ever underestimate the importance you can have because history has shown us that courage can be contagious and hope can take on a life of its own"

— **Michelle Obama**

This chapter highlights cultural change, social impact, and civil rights models that could be leveraged to begin embedding a racial equity approach to how you build a healthy community and workforce. It takes courage to dedicate your life and career to improving racial equity for everyone. Here are a few frameworks to get you started.

Diversity & Inclusion Models

The Diversity Equity & Inclusion practice continues to grow and evolve. Unfortunately, sometimes the DEI industry is seen as the profession where you can see no results, get nothing done, and keep your job because you made a "good faith" effort. However, the industry continues to fight for more credibility, and since the 90s has been adding models that could be used to better address systemic racism. These models have helped DEI move further away from the soft skill, feel-good industry, to a more mature practice.

One of my favorite DEI models is the Miller-Katz Model. This framework provides a rigorous approach to uncovering and solving some of the problems related to DEI, and it would be great for specifically addressing anti-Black racism. The Miller and Katz's Exclusive Club to Inclusion Organization model is one of the best at helping leaders honestly and accurately assess their current state. Companies have made promises and pledges to improve the Black experience of their workplace, but how do they know where to start? If you don't know your current state, you might be beginning the wrong initiatives. This model outlines five stages on the inclusion continuum - An Exclusive Club/Passive Club, Symbolic Differences, Critical Mass, Welcoming, and Inclusive Organization. While this model is usually run in the context of general DEI themes, how would your organization fare if the assessment was focused solely on racial equity? Just because you believe your company's current DEI state is welcoming to diverse groups, or you have been recognized with a top 50 DE&I company award every year, doesn't necessarily mean you

From Promises to Progress

have an anti-racist workplace culture. Here is how I would reimagine this model with an anti-racism approach:[91]

Stage 1: Exclusive/Passive Club: These are the organizations that don't see color or differences. When pushed, they revert to All Lives Matter, or We Are One Human Race rhetoric in an attempt to sidestep or dismiss racial issues. They have very little Black representation, and their actions show they are determined to maintain the status quo.

Stage 2: Symbolic Differences: They have some Black representation, but the exclusive culture remains the same. Their few Black leaders have limited power. They made a Black Lives Matter statement in 2020, and some may even already have a Black employee resource group and Black History Month celebrations. These organizations are either at the learning stage or purposely giving the illusion of inclusion.

Stage 3: Critical Mass: This is the most challenging stage, and it includes a great deal of tolerance and transformation. This is the stage we hope many organizations have evolved to post-George Floyd Movement. To grow past this stage, it takes a long-term plan, not one-off events. This is where the guardians of the status quo feel threatened because the company begins to recognize the need to support their Black colleagues fully. They acknowledge things need to improve, but they haven't started implementing real change yet.

---

[91] The Kaleel Jamison Consulting Group. Chttps://copdei.extension.org/wp-content/uploads/2019/06/The-Path-from-Exclusive-Club.pdf

Stage 4: Welcoming: They have moved toward acknowledging that some of their corporate systems negatively impact their Black colleagues, communities, and customers. Everyone feels safe speaking up to address anti-Black systems in the company and often sees action when they speak up.

Stage 5: Inclusive Organization: The stage where Black culture is fully valued. All their talents, skills, and energy are leveraged. Change is constant, and these organizations are well-positioned to adapt to race-related issues that arise inside and outside of the organization. These organizations continue to examine and address issues of power and privilege in society and their organization.

Which stage above would most resemble your organization?

Employee Engagement Survey Assessments

The second framework I recommend repurposing comes from the field of employee engagement. The Gallup Organization defines employee engagement as employees being involved in, enthusiastic about, and committed to their work and workplace. Gallup's 50 years of research shows when organizations go beyond mere satisfaction and have engaged employees, companies can leverage untapped potential resulting in better business outcomes. Gallup designed an employee engagement framework and survey called the Q12. You don't have to use Gallup's survey, but a good employee survey is a must. The importance of the survey design is often underestimated.

Their survey consists of 12 questions that aim to measure the most critical 12 elements of employee engagement.[92]

Beyond the survey, the Q12 would be an excellent framework for your Anti-Racism Taskforce to build from. For each Q12 Question item below, I repurposed these proven 12 elements of the employee engagement framework as the 12 elements of the Black employee experience.

The Q12 consists of the following questions in bold.[93] Examples of a Black experience approach are in italics:

1 **I know what is expected of me at work.**

- *Do Black employees know when to escalate issues related to unfairness and discrimination? Where and how to escalate them, and what to expect?*

2 **I have the materials and equipment I need to do my work right.**

- *Do the departments/stores located in predominately Black communities or with majority Black employees have the same access to resources as other locations. Are the materials/equipment needed for success distributed equitably?*

---

[92] Gallup, Inc. "How to Improve Employee Engagement in the Workplace - Gallup." Gallup.com, November 14, 2022. https://www.gallup.com/workplace/285674/improve-employee-engagement-workplace.aspx.
[93] Gallup, Inc. "Gallup's Q12 Employee Engagement Survey - Gallup." Gallup.com, November 14, 2022. https://www.gallup.com/workplace/356063/gallup-q12-employee-engagement-survey.aspx.

3. At work, I have the opportunity to do what I do best every day.

　⊙ *Does your Black talent feel like they could bring their authentic self to work?*

4. In the last seven days, I have received recognition or praise for doing good work.

　⊙ *Review your monthly, quarterly, and annual recognition awards. Are Black employees disproportionately left out of awards/recognition?*

5. My supervisor, or someone at work, seems to care about me as a person.

　⊙ *Are your managers held accountable when treating their employees unfairly?*

6. There is someone at work who encourages my development.

　⊙ *Do you have formal mentoring, networking, or sponsorship programs to support the development of Black colleagues?*

7. At work, my opinions seem to count.

　⊙ *After gathering feedback from your Black colleagues at town halls, virtual conferences, and team meetings, did you act on the feedback?*

8   The mission or purpose of my company makes me feel my job is important.

- *What has your company done to fight against anti-Black racism in society? What risk or stance has your company taken before and after the murder of George Floyd?*

9   My associates or fellow employees are committed to doing quality work.

- *Are your colleagues committed to addressing anti-Black racism in and outside of the workplace, or is it just an employee volunteer activity?*

10 I have a best friend at work.

- *When catastrophes like the murder of Trayvon Martin, Tamir Rice, the mass shooting in Buffalo, and other tragic events happen, will Black colleagues feel alone and isolated? Or do Black colleagues feel they have a safe place to talk?*

11 In the last six months, someone at work has talked to me about my progress.

- *Feedback is a gift. Are managers trained to provide constructive feedback to diverse employees?*

12 I have had opportunities at work to learn and grow.

- *Are Black employees getting access to stretch assignments at the same rate as others?*

The Q12 framework has been used to drive cultural change within many Fortune 500 companies. Couldn't this be used to improve the Black experience in the workplace? The goal is to have a place where Black Americans can work to their full potential, and where Black employees are proud to work, and willing to go above and beyond on the job. An environment that results in less absenteeism, turnover, and higher productivity and attracts Black talent.

There are many frameworks to choose from in the disciplines of Corporate Citizenship, Diversity & Inclusion, Employee Engagement, and Change Management. You may want to consider other effective models: Deloitte's D&I Maturity Model, Hubbard's DRIO Model, and Dr. Roosevelt Thomas Jr.'s Strategic Diversity Management. Organizational change initiatives take dedicated time and energy from your team. This is not an "off the side of the desk" assignment or a non-paid extracurricular activity. Whether you use this model or a different one, you need to use an effective task force dedicated to transforming your organization's culture.

United Nations Sustainable Development Goals (UNSDG)

The United Nations Sustainable Development Goals (UNSDG) provide an excellent framework for companies to use in their fight to make the world a better place. It takes a systems approach to solving colossal world problems. The UNSDGs are widely known in Corporate Social Responsibility, Corporate Citizenship, and Social Impact professional circles, but not too far beyond this field. This is a blueprint and a set of goals guided by measurable indicators and targets committed by United Nations members to pursue a truly sustainable and equitable world by 2030. The framework was designed by a special collaboration of great minds from all over the world, and it is made up of 17 goals, 169 goal targets, and 230 related indicators.

The 17 goals include: 1. No Poverty, 2. Zero Hunger, 3. Good Health and Well-being, 4. Quality Education, 5. Gender Equality, 6. Clean Water and Sanitation, 7. Affordable and Clean Energy, 8. Decent Work and Economic Growth, 9. Industry, Innovation and Infrastructure, 10. Reduced Inequalities, 11. Sustainable Cities and Communities, 12. Responsible Consumption and Production, 13. Climate Change, 14. Life Below Water, 15. Life on Land, 16. Peace, Justice, and Strong Institutions, and 17. Partnerships.

Some large companies are already using the UNSDG as the framework to build their Corporate Social Responsibility Strategic plan. Companies usually don't select all 17 sustainable development goals. Instead, they choose a handful of goals they are best positioned to impact directly. For example, if your company is a health system, you would most likely adopt Goal #3, Good Health & Well-being as one of your goals.[94][95]

---

[94] **The Society for the Psychological Study of Social Issue. Psychology Coalition at the United Nations.** https://sustainabledevelopment.un.org/content/documents/14989RacismPost2015SDGAdvocacyDoc526.pdf

[95] **United Nations. un.org,** https://www.un.org/sustainabledevelopment/sustainable-development-goals/

Racial Equity Audits

Conducting a racial equity audit is one of the most important actions a company could take in the fight to close the racial equity gap. There has been a rise in these racial equity or civil right audits among U.S. companies. First led by Laura Murphy's audits of Facebook and Airbnb,[96] and now many others after 2020 have either already conducted an audit or have committed to doing so. According the Reuters, Amazon will also be conducting a racial equity audit of its hourly workers after facing pressure from shareholders.[97] The Bloomberg Law article, "Racial Equity Audits: The New ESG Frontier" highlighted this push for more audits, "Investors and stakeholders are paying greater attention to environmental, social, and governance (ESG) impacts of public companies. Increasingly, they are requesting, if not demanding, that companies consider civil rights and social justice issues, often through racial equity audits."[98]

This rise in the demand for audits is a positive sign of racial equity being embedded in the business. What gets measured gets done. However, companies taking this first step towards equity must understand the audit is not the end point. The audit informs the plan of action and holds companies accountable for the follow through.

---

[96] Murphy, Laura. "The Rationale for and Key Elements of a Business Civil Rights Audit." 2021. http://civilrightsdocs.info/pdf/reports/Civil-Rights-Audit-Report-2021.pdf

[97] Sloan, Karen, and Karen Sloan. "Paul Weiss Bets on Racial Equality Audits with New Practice Led by Loretta Lynch." Reuters, July 19, 2022. https://www.reuters.com/legal/legalindustry/paul-weiss-bets-racial-equality-audits-with-new-practice-led-by-loretta-lynch-2022-07-19/.

[98] McDowell, Valecia, and Elena Mitchell. "Racial Equity Audits: The New ESG Frontier," April 26, 2022. https://news.bloomberglaw.com/esg/racial-equity-audits-the-new-esg-frontier.

From Promises to Progress

Laura Murphy, most notable for her highly profiled audits of Facebook and Airbnb, defined civil rights audits in her report, *The Rationale for and Key Elements of a Business Civil Right Audit* as, "An independent, systemic examination of significant civil rights and racial equity issues that may exist in a company and provided a plan of action to address those issues in a thorough, deliberative, timely, and transparent manner. Auditors with civil rights expertise will assess a company's business policies, practices, products, and services to determine whether and how those components have a discriminatory effect and/or disparate impact on people historically subject to discrimination. After an initial assessment, the auditors work with the company to issue a public report to provide a blueprint for corrective action and provocative, equitable outcomes, and to ensure that structures are in place to implement civil rights changes and prevent civil rights harms."[99]

There isn't one single correct way to conduct a racial equity audit. The scope and depth of the audit would depend on the size and maturity of the organization. What's most important is that it is conducted by an independent, external organization. Sometimes these audits are led by a civil rights law firm, civil rights non-profit, or a DEI consulting group.

---

[99] Murphy, Laura. "The Rationale for and Key Elements of a Business Civil Rights Audit." 2021. http://civilrightsdocs.info/pdf/reports/Civil-Rights-Audit-Report-2021.pdf

"When delivering a high-quality racial equity audit, it's important the entire organization understands the vision, purpose and initial desired outcomes for the audit" said Rick Huntley, 20 year DEI consultant and co-author of *Journeys of Race, Color & Culture: From Racial Inequality to Equity and Inclusion*, "An example of a racial equity audit I conducted with a private sector organization was a combination of focus groups, individual interviews with senior leaders and an electronic survey. The audit is a discovery process, which enabled the organization to a snapshot of itself as a starting point to facilitate change toward racial equity. Staff must be deeply assured of the confidentiality and the anonymity of the audit. All must feel at ease to share and not wondering whether there might be retribution for their comments. For this reason, having an independent vendor often helps lessen any fears that might be present." Huntley continued, "The audit must not be a stand-alone. When you start the audit, you are making a commitment to the organization, and they are then awaiting next steps."

Laura Murphy, also provided ten key recommendations for conducting civil rights and racial equity audits. These recommendations are based on her experience conducting audits for Airbnb, Facebook, and Starbucks:[100]

---

[100] Murphy, Laura. "The Rationale for and Key Elements of a Business Civil Rights Audit." 2021. http://civilrightsdocs.info/pdf/reports/Civil-Rights-Audit-Report-2021.pdf

1. Have the support and active engagement of senior executives, including the CEO and board of directors.
2. Be rooted in U.S. civil rights law, focusing on race, gender, and other protected classes.
3. Have an established purpose within a company and a shared understanding of why an audit is being conducted.
4. Be led by an independent person or firm with deep expertise in civil rights and racial justice as well as adequate resources to complete the audit.
5. Identify the various external and internal challenges facing the company.
6. Be supported by a team of executives and staff who will make sure the auditor has access to the company's policies, practices, products and services through the review for their potential discriminatory impact.
7. Result in a clear plan of action.
8. Publicly state the findings in a report that identifies civil rights concerns and addresses the areas where the company has or will take action.
9. Have a clear timeline.
10. Involve consultation with stakeholders throughout the process, including civil rights advocates and organizations.

Putting it into action

These are just a few models and frameworks that could be used to implement real change. It's important to know that you don't have to reinvent the wheel. There are tools already available to use. Secondly, there is value in starting with a model or framework that many others are familiar with. It provides credibility and provides a common language when you're working together in teams to solve problems.

Questions for Reflection

1. What models and frameworks have you used to drive culture change or any change management at your company?

2. What stage of the Miller Katz model best resembles your organization in this repurposed version? Why?

3. Answer all of the questions in the Employee Engagement Section (Q1-12)

4. Which UN Sustainable Development Goals could your organization best support? Why?

5. What have you learned from Laura Murphy's racial equity audits of Airbnb and Facebook?

Chapter 9

Putting It into Action

The universe doesn't give you what you ask for with your thoughts; it gives you what you demand with your actions

— **Dr. Steve Maraboli**

Frameworks and models can't do the work for you. They are only tools. If you don't have a dedicated team to put the tool to work, having the best tool in the world is useless. The leadership team must be ready to be trailblazers. There aren't many who have seriously taken on the task of combating anti-Black racism in the workplace at the executive level. Unfortunately, quite often these efforts are farmed out to the mid-level employees who joined a Business Resource Group.

It's Not the Business Resource Group's Responsibility

Who should be responsible for leading the work to address anti-Black racism at your organization? Is it your Black Business Resource Groups (BRG), also known as Employee Resource Groups (ERG), or Affinity Group? Some organizations have been handing this responsibility off to the BRGs, but this is not fair. BRG should play a role and add value in the fight to combat anti-Black racism, but it should not be their responsibility.

Members of BRGs are volunteering (unpaid) outside of their work assignments. These volunteer groups usually focus on social events, leadership development, networking, and Black History Month events. BRGs are the place where groups with similar backgrounds help organizations create a sense of belonging for colleagues by creating opportunities for them to connect, and they also give allies opportunities to gain cultural awareness. Some BRGs even take the extra step by contributing to the actual business by participating in focus groups, surveys, diversity recruiting, diverse interview panels, reviewing advertising campaigns, and more. Leveraging Black colleagues' perspectives to support the business is a smart strategy, but executives take it too far when they think they can hand off the crucial task of combating anti-Black racism in the workplace to a volunteer group.

If a volunteer group had the power to remove the barriers related to racism from the workplace, it would have been done 50 years ago when BRGs first started. BRGs, specifically Black BRGs, have been more of a training ground to help Black colleagues navigate their way through racism, not end racism. Many Black BRGs provide tips on addressing microaggressions, finding white executive allies to mentor and sponsor you, getting visible assignments as a volunteer when you are being blocked from stretch-work assignments, and learning from other Black colleagues that made it up the ranks. All are valuable for the individual, but don't change the system. These

BRG groups are not designed to create a sustainable change of the policies and practices at an organization.

BRGs are never assigned to lead any other major system or structural changes. For example, it's unlikely any of them were ever appointed to design what hybrid work during the pandemic would look like, they are not managing mergers and acquisitions, nor do they select the organization's Board of Directors. So why would a CEO think it's okay to entirely hand off the responsibility of something as crucial to the success of an organization as building an anti-racist culture? The BRG didn't make the promises and pledges, the CEO did. If the promises of combating anti-Black racism in the workplace and society really mattered to them, they wouldn't ask a group of unpaid volunteers to lead this along with their regular full-time work assignment. This is a red flag that the executive leadership isn't serious about change, and it is a formula for failure.

The "pass it to the BRG" strategy is unsustainable. When members get new challenging work assignments from their regular 9 to 5 work, get promoted to a new role, or when it's just a busy time of the year, the first assignments to get dropped are the volunteer activities. Rightly so, they prioritize the actual job they were hired to perform.

Successful Racial Equity Is Not a "Nice-to-Have"; It's a Must-Have. Hire Someone to Lead it!

These volunteer groups are excellent for one-off or short assignments, but not for leading sustainable change. According to the HBR article, "What Black Employee Resources Need Right Now", Amazon found a way to get their BRG involved in shorter assignments. The article states, "In the wake of George Floyd's death, Amazon committed $10 million to fight for social justice and aiding Black communities. The Company's Black Employee Network (BEN) helped leadership identify the recipients of those funds." Here, Amazon did not shift the responsibility. They only sought help from the BRG.

In the same article, Doordash is highlighted for establishing a $500,000 fund directed by its Black ERG.[101] According to Doordash's site, they are donating $1 million, with $500k going to Black Lives Matter and $500k to create a fund directed by the Black@Doordash ERG towards state and local organizations.[102] I love Doordash's creativity and the $1 million pledge plan, however I am concerned about its sustainability. Impact investing is more than just writing a check and walking away. It involves researching and vetting nonprofits, and measuring the impact of the dollars donated. Not just Doordash, but all companies need to hire someone to do this job.

---

[101] Harvard Business Review. "What Black Employee Resource Groups Need Right Now," July 15, 2020. https://hbr.org/2020/06/what-black-employee-resource-groups-need-right-now.
[102] "DoorDash Merchant Support," n.d. https://help.doordash.com/merchants/s/article/Standing-Together-for-Justice?language=en_US.

Putting It into Action

BRGs should be there to help direct the dollars, not to own the directing of dollars. Building a long-term, equitable system of community giving should not be outsourced to a volunteer group. Give this task to the Director of Philanthropy, and if you don't have one, it is time to hire someone.

I'm not the only one concerned about assigning these crucial business tasks to unpaid volunteers. To remedy the problem, some companies are considering paying people for their BRG work. In a blog post from September 2020, Twitter recognized the work of BRG chairs is essential to Twitter's success and that it is not a "side hustle" or "volunteer activity". They introduced a new compensation program to recognize the global leadership team of BRGs formally.[103] Adding additional incentives to recognize and reward internal volunteer work is good, but it doesn't solve the main problem which is shifting responsibility to volunteers. A 2020 Washington Post article also described the increase in these "volunteer assignments". It explained how companies began relying on BRGs to host panels on race, vet company statements, allocate donations to racial justice nonprofits, and manage new diversity initiatives.[104] Compensating BRG volunteers for attempting to drive anti-racism programs across the organizations will not improve the results. There are no shortcuts. If the program or initiative matters, if the Black experience matters,

---

[103] "Inclusion & Diversity Report September 2020: #BlackLivesMatter," n.d. https://blog.twitter.com/en_us/topics/company/2020/inclusion-and-diversity-report-blacklivesmatter-september-2020.

[104] Tiku, Nitasha. "Tech companies are asking their black employee groups to fix Silicon Valley's race problem – often for free" June, 26, 2020. https://www.washingtonpost.com/technology/2020/06/26/black-ergs-tech/

start by hiring someone to do the work or making it a part of someone's actual full-time job.

Another reason why BRGs owning systemic change hasn't been successful is that it has been too risky for their careers. When your career is in I.T., accounting, marketing, etc., it could be perceived by leadership in your department that you are moonlighting as a diversity & inclusion professional and not giving the extra effort to your actual job. In addition, it also gives employees the illusion of Black people in leadership. The 2020 Washington Post article mentioned above also highlighted these potential issues. During the height of the summer's civil unrest, they interviewed current and former leaders of employee resource groups of Black, Latino, LGBTQ, and Women, and they said, "They (ERG Leaders) welcome the visibility and access to upper management. But they worry these programs can give business leaders a pass on diversity by allowing them to demonstrate support for minority groups without diversifying the people in charge. And some say pushing for change can hurt their careers." [105]

In conclusion, BRGs don't have the power, they do not get paid for their work, and it's risky for their career to push for systemic changes. How could real change happen when the real people in power could block their efforts by hurting their careers? BRG leads are forced to be super brave and many times sacrifice their careers. In this situation, everyone loses. The business doesn't meet their

---

[105] Tiku, Nitasha. "Tech companies are asking their black employee groups to fix Silicon Valley's race problem – often for free" June, 26, 2020.
https://www.washingtonpost.com/technology/2020/06/26/black-ergs-tech/

Putting It into Action

commitments, BRG leaders are burnt out, and Black employee experience doesn't improve.

The Executive Task Force

Salesforce, the American Cloud-Based software company, set an excellent example of what the anti-racism task force structure could look like. They put together a special Racial Equality Justice Taskforce in response to the civil unrest after the murder of George Floyd. The taskforce consists of Tony Prophet (Chief Equality and Recruiting Officer), Ebony Beckwith (Chief Philanthropic Officer), Craig Cuffie (Chief Procurement Officer), and Eric Loeb (EVP, Government Affairs). Their plan has systemic change goals in four pillars - employee, philanthropy, purchasing, and policy - and they have people with the power in all four focus areas to see it through. For the Employee Focus, here are a few of the proposed systemic changes:

- First, they are working with a third-party consulting firm to assess all of the people processes. Having an audit of your culture, policies, and practices is a great start.
- Secondly, they are building a standardized inclusion promotion process and training required for managers to complete ahead of promotions.
- The third significant change will be revamping their scorecard program. This will allow senior leaders to detail headcount, hiring, attrition, and promotion data by gender and race to drive accountability.

Salesforce published a report one year later, in May 2021. It did not include an update on the progress of the scorecard and standardized inclusion promotion process, but they made gains in their goal to increase Black representation. They moved from 3.0% to 3.9%. They saw the most progress over the year in Black hiring by doubling the percentage from 4.0% to 8.1%, which they attribute to their new diversity recruiting team, interview training, and employee referral process.[106]

The Leadership Team Matters

Taking on this endeavor requires a team with strong leadership attributes: influence, determination, and credibility.

This team must have influence: the ability to socialize the systemic changes across the organization and get buy-in.

Secondly, they need the determination to follow through and execute this long and challenging task. Bringing major policy and program changes to an organization isn't for the faint of heart.

And lastly, the team must be credible. It's extremely important for this team to be trusted morally. It's one thing to have the skills, talent, and power to implement culture change and enterprise-wide initiatives, but when it comes to social justice, the spotlight is even brighter on the individuals' values and moral compass. Integrity, compassion, and courage means the world.

---

[106] Salesforce.com. "Racial Equality and Justice Taskforce," n.d. https://www.salesforce.com/company/equality/racial-equality-justice-taskforce/.

Questions for Reflection

1. What role did your organization's Black BRG play in the workplace events following the murder of George Floyd?

2. What role do you want the BRG to play in the advancement of racial equity and addressing anti-Black racism?

3. How would you rate your executive team's influence, determination, and credibility? And why?

Appendix

2020-2021 List of Corporate Racial Equity Actions

2020-2021 has given DEI, Corporate Social Responsibility and other corporate professionals a great opportunity to enact change. It has been a chance for purpose-driven organizations to grab a hold of the momentum and propel their company forward to real, sustainable, racial equity in the workplace.

2020 Actions to Address Anti-Black Racism Statements and Commitments

Mckinsey and company's report on the top 1000 US companies found the following actions between May 25 – October 31, 2020:

- 32% made statements
- 22% made external commitments
- 18% made internal commitments.

A couple hundred companies out of the thousand made financial commitments to help the community address racial inequities, and a smaller percentage of companies committed to improving their internal systemic issues.[107] It may have felt like every company was taking some action, but the majority of companies didn't make a statement or commitment. However, racial equity was still higher on the radar than ever before.

Crisis Management

Many companies jumped right into crisis management. They showed empathy by acknowledging that Derek Chauvin's actions were wrong and that systemic racism is real. They provided safe places for employees to express their pain and even admitted the need to improve the Black experience within their own company. They used constant communication, talked about transparency, conducted employee surveys, virtual town halls and celebrated Juneteenth.

$50 Billion Pledges

U.S. companies pledged over $50 billion toward racial equity efforts, but only a small percentage has reached the community. According to Creative Investment Research, only $250 million has been spent or committed a year later. Less than 1% of the pledges have been made in a year.

Even with this slow rollout, it is too soon for the public to cry foul. Most of the commitments are multi-year, and I would rather have companies and nonprofits thoughtfully use the funds instead of

---

[107] Liu, Amy, and Reniya Dinkins. "From Commitments to Action: How CEOs Can Advance Racial Equity in Their Regional Economies." Brookings, March 11, 2021. https://www.brookings.edu/essay/from-commitments-to-action-how-ceos-can-advance-racial-equity-in-their-regional-economies/.

rushing to spend the money.[108] Not to mention, only $4.2 Billion of the $50 Billion were actually grants. Much of the funds pledged from the financial institutions were in the form of loans and investments, were banks aim to profit.[109] Loans and investments aren't a bad way to support the Black community, it's just that these large $1 Billion - marketing and public relations driven - headlines were intentionally misleading.

Promise Trackers

The addition of public tracking was also a significant change in the system. We now have groups tracking all of the pledges and promises made by organizations. JUST Capital, founded in 2013 by Paul Tudor Jones, Deepak Chopra, and others, focuses on helping companies improve how they serve all their stakeholders. This organization built the Corporate Racial Equity Tracker, where you can explore the commitments and actions by industry and company.[110] The Aspen Institute, a global nonprofit organization whose mission is the commitment to realizing a free, just, and equitable society, is also

---

[108] Quiroz-Gutierrez, Marco. "American Companies Pledged $50 Billion to Black Communities. Most of It Hasn't Materialized." Fortune, May 6, 2021. https://fortune.com/2021/05/06/us-companies-black-communities-money-50-billion/.
[109] Jan, Tracy Jena McGregor. "After George Floyd's Death, Big Business Pledged Nearly $50 Billion for Racial Justice. This Is Where the Money Is Going." Washington Post, August 23, 2021. https://www.washingtonpost.com/business/interactive/2021/george-floyd-corporate-america-racial-justice/.
[110] JUST Capital. https://justcapital.com/about/

Appendix

keeping an eye on organizations with a tracker called the Anti-Racism pledge tracker.[111]

With the implementation of Just Capital, Aspen Institute's anti-racism tracker, and many other trackers, we now have a system in place to hold these CEOs' feet to the fire... somewhat. These organizations can't make companies follow through, but they will be able to at least identify the CEOs who made big promises but didn't follow through.

Tracking organizations shouldn't forget about the silent CEOs. We can't forget about the 68% of the Fortune 1000 companies that were quiet during the summer of 2020. Silence wasn't an option for the large companies, but many mid-sized and small companies purposely slid under the radar. Did they quietly take action to improve racial equity or did they just ignore the problem?

Neither can we forget about the CEOs who made racist comments. Some CEOs refused to recognize that Black lives matter and refused to acknowledge the injustice against George Floyd. There was the former CEO of Crossfit, George Glassman, who was caught saying, "We're not mourning for George Floyd – I don't think me or any of my staff are." Glassman was held accountable and removed from his CEO position.[112] We have to hold everyone accountable – the pledgers, the silent, and the overtly racist CEOs.

---

[111] Aspen Institute. "The Aspen Digital Anti-Racism Pledge Tracker". June 25, 2020 https://www.aspeninstitute.org/blog-posts/aspen-digital-anti-racism-pledge-tracker/
[112] Gorman, Alyx, and Josh Taylor. "CrossFit CEO Greg Glassman Resigns after Offensive George Floyd and Coronavirus Tweets." The Guardian, July 1, 2020.

American Optimism

Another major change has been American optimism that action would be taken to address anti-Black racism. Searmount.com has been tracking the perspectives of employees and the new actions by companies since the murder of George Floyd. According to Searmount's findings, employees perceived the pledges and statements their companies made as authentic - 88% of White employees and 85% of Black employees. Employees, and most people in the U.S., believed this time was different. Most people still think this was a great awakening like no other, and companies are serious about change. Black employees are confident that progress will be made. Seramount says in 2021 only 16% of Black employees say their company is all talk.[113]

The confidence and optimism around racial equity in the workplace was at an all-time high, but the research that soon followed was less optimistic. According to the "From Pledge to Progress" report, "While almost all executives say they are committed to helping their companies fight racism in their organizations, a third of those who agree they committed to fighting racism say they feel forced to support anti-racism efforts. And a staggering 79 percent of those who agree they are committed say they think corporate efforts on DE&I are overblown."

---

https://www.theguardian.com/us-news/2020/jun/10/greg-glassman-crossfit-ceo-resigns-george-floyd-protest-coronavirus-tweets-conspiracy-theories.
[113] Searmount "From Pledge to Progress: Corporate America One Year After George Floyd's Death" 2020. https://assets.bonniercorp.com/pdfs/Pledge_to_Progress.pdf

Appendix

If these executive attitudes worry you, you are not alone. This is a recipe for a lot of heartbreak. The public is optimistic about organizations genuinely wanting to address systemic racism, but many executives feel like they are doing something unnecessary.[114]

Race for DEI roles

The last major change a year later was the boost in Diversity & Inclusion roles. There was an increase in D&I positions, D&I consultants, and D&I/racial bias training. Corporations saw the urgency to bring in employees with the knowledge and expertise to address anti-Black racism in society and within the company.

Conclusion

A good list of items has been accomplished in one year. They include the resurgence in the field of DE&I, companies taking public stances against social injustice, greater commitments to employees and the community, and better monitoring systems. However, I am still concerned about the sustainability of these efforts. If changes to the system, framework, and structural racism against Black people haven't changed, it will be easy for companies to quickly change its course.

---

[114] Searmount "From Pledge to Progress: Corporate America One Year After George Floyd's Death" 2020. https://assets.bonniercorp.com/pdfs/Pledge_to_Progress.pdf

Questions for Reflection

1 What were the biggest advancements in racial equity you've witnesses or participated in since 2020?

2 Are you as optimistic that companies are going to continue their efforts to combat anti-Black racism as you were in 2020? Why?

3 How is your company doing on its pledges and promises?

4 How has the DEI department changed at you company? Any new leaders and programs, or greater influence and power?

Acknowledgements

During the actual composition of this book, I have been greatly helped by the discussions I had with family, friends, DEI practitioners and other corporate leaders.

Thank you to all of the corporate leaders, nonprofit leaders, and DEI practitioners that took time out of their busy schedule to speak with me: Alida Miranda-Wolff, Allison Manswell, Bama Althreya, Eboni Riley, Jana Simon, Jess Evora, Louis Montgomery, Lynn Orosco, Nat Alston, Rick Huntley, Robert Foster, Ronnie Dunn, Sukari Pinnock, Tony Torian, and the JP Morgan Chase interns.

Special thank you to those that encouraged me to begin writing and to keep writing: Nakia Green, Donnie Bedney, Jeri Wright, Telie Woods, Wayne "Lyte" Brown, Olivia Fernandez, and many others.

This work could not be done without great editors and writing coaches. Thank you, Theresa Spencer, Reginald Beamon, Nikki West, and others that took the time to read all of the early versions of my manuscript, and provide coaching and feedback.

Thank you to my mother, Nadine Grubbs, for all her love and support! My father, Milton Beamon, for his guidance and support! And my step-father, E.J Grubbs, thank you for the encouragement to create this work, and designing an awesome book cover for me.

Special acknowledges again to everyone who assisted in the development of this book through editing, proofreading, coaching, interviews, advice and encouragement.

About the Author

Andrew Beamon is an experienced professional in Corporate Social Responsibility, Racial Equity, Human Resource Strategy and Economic Development.

Prior to joining TD Bank Group to lead the U.S. Corporate Citizenship Colleague Engagement Programs, he worked as the Director of Field Operations for the SCORE Association, and as a Human Capital Consultant with The Gallup Organization.

Andrew earned his bachelor's degree in business with a concentration in hospitality and tourism administration from North Carolina Central University in Durham, North Carolina, and his master's degree in organizational psychology from the University of Hartford in Hartford, Connecticut. He completed Georgetown's Strategic Diversity & Inclusion Management Executive Certification and Boston College's Certification in Strategic Corportate Citizenship Management.

Currently resides back in his hometown, Waterbury, Connecticut

Visit him at *www.andrewbeamon.com*

Made in United States
Orlando, FL
29 January 2023

29137141R00095